D1515925

# BACKROADS OF

## More terrific books about Florida from Gulf Publishing Company:

Camper's Guide to Florida Parks, Trails, Rivers, and Beaches

Beachcomber's Guide to Gulf Coast Marine Life

Florida Historical Markers and Sites

Fish Florida: Saltwater

Mariner's Atlas: Florida Gulf Coast and the Florida Keys

Mariner's Atlas: Southeast Florida and the Florida Keys

Diving and Snorkeling Guide to Florida's East Coast, 2nd Edition

Diving and Snorkeling Guide to the Florida Keys

**Gulf Publishing Company**
Houston, Texas

# BACKROADS OF
# FLORIDA

*Ann Ruff*

## DEDICATION

To Richard Wright, Rosie Veggerberg, and Judy
Marshall, for traveling the backroads of Florida
with me.

## BACKROADS OF FLORIDA

Copyright © 1992 by Gulf Publishing Company, Houston,
Texas. All rights reserved. Printed in the United States of
America. This book, or parts thereof, may not be reproduced
in any form without permission of the publisher.

Gulf Publishing Company
P.O. Box 2608
Houston, Texas 77252-2608

10  9  8  7  6  5  4  3  2  1

**Library of Congress Cataloging-in-Publication Data**

Ruff, Ann, 1930–
 Backroads of Florida/Ann Ruff.
  p. cm.
 Includes index.
 **ISBN 0-88415-008-9**
 1. Florida—Description and travel—1981—Guide-books.
 2. Automobile travel—Florida—Guide-books. I. Title.
 F309.3.R84   1992
 917.5904'63—dc20                                        91-29924
                                                              CIP

# CONTENTS

ACKNOWLEDGMENTS ............................... vii

INTRODUCTION ...................................... viii

MORE ABOUT FLORIDA ............................. ix

HISTORY ................................................. 1

FLORIDA MAP .......................................... 9

NORTHWEST FLORIDA ............................. 11
  Tallahassee—Apalachicola—Blountstown, 12
  Tallahassee—Havana, 21
  Tallahassee—Cedar Key, 21
  Tallahassee—White Springs, 26
  Pensacola—Milton, 29
  Panama City—DeFuniak Springs—Marianna, 31

NORTHEAST FLORIDA ............................... 38
  Jacksonville—Amelia Island, 40
  Jacksonville—St. Augustine and Marineland, 42
  Jacksonville—Palatka (St. Johns River Drive), 47
  Gainesville—Rawlings Home—Micanopy—
    McIntosh, 51

v

**CENTRAL WEST FLORIDA** .......................... **55**

St. Petersburg—Homosassa Springs—Inverness—
  Brooksville—Tampa, 56
Tampa—Sarasota—Arcadia—Zolfo Springs, 71
Sarasota—Venice—Englewood, 75

**CENTRAL FLORIDA** ................................... **79**

Orlando—Winter Park—Sanford—Wekiwa
  Springs, 84
Orlando—Mt. Dora—Ocala, 88
Orlando—Lakeland—Lake Wales, 95

**CENTRAL EAST FLORIDA** .......................... **103**

Daytona—Ponce Inlet Lighthouse, 106
Daytona—Cassadaga—De Leon Springs, 108

**SOUTHWEST FLORIDA** ............................. **113**

Fort Myers—Captiva Island—Sanibel Island, 115
Fort Myers—Port Charlotte—Boca Grande, 118
Fort Myers—Naples—Everglades City, 122

**SOUTHEAST FLORIDA** ............................. **129**

Out and Around Miami, 131
Miami—Clewiston—Okeechobee, 144
Biscayne National Park, 150

**FLORIDA KEYS AND KEY WEST** .................. **152**

**INDEX** ................................................. **173**

# ACKNOWLEDGMENTS

The Florida tourist bureaus that I worked with were among the most helpful in the world. I am deeply indebted to them, and particularly to Martha Thomas of the Tourism Division of the Florida Department of Commerce. She paved the way for this book, and I owe her a special thank you. Also, among the wonderful people were Georgia Carter of Destination Daytona, Jill DeChello of SeaEscape, William Puckett of Marineland, Marcheta Brewer of Orlando Convention & Visitors Bureau, Ellen Kennedy of Lee County, Lee Daniels of Pinellas Suncoast, Lorraine Moore and all the gorgeous gals of Geiger & Associates, terrific Warren Zeller of Florida City, Jean Gomez of Florida Keys and Key West, Nanci Yuronis of Grand Romance, Susan Linder of Naples Chamber of Commerce, Stacy Rossiter of Tampa Convention & Visitors Bureau, and the Zimmerman Agency.

And, to all these great B&B inns and super hotels, many thanks for your generous hospitality: The Reach in Key West; Peabody Hotel in Orlando, and Sonya Snyder; the Hiltons in Tampa, Orlando, and Clearwater; Holiday Inn, Osprey; 'Tween Waters Inn, Captiva Island; Hampton Inn, Florida City, and Terry Jordan; Pelican Inn, Dog Island; Peppermill, Monticello; 1875 House, Amelia Island; Seven Sisters Inn, Ocala; Pink Camellia, Apalachicola; Chalet Suzanne, Lake Wales; The Lakeside Inn, Mt. Dora; Adventures, Inc., Milton; Pirate's Cove, Daytona; Park Plaza, Winter Park; Banyan House, Venice; and Inn by the Sea, Naples.

# INTRODUCTION

Florida is a fascinating state, and far more than just beaches and sunshine and Disney World. From the dark piney woods in north Florida to the swamps of the Everglades, I discovered a myriad of backroad treasures.

My favorite places were those referred to as "Old Florida" and "Natural Florida." By some miracle, these scenic sites and archaic attractions escaped the developers' bulldozers and add a special ambiance to a state known for its golf courses and posh resorts.

Especially delightful were the historic inns and hotels that have been restored. Many were tucked away in little towns and on hidden beaches, and I wanted to stay in them all.

Florida is working hard to preserve its remaining natural beauty: the state parks are all well planned and most offer a bit of Florida as it was when Ponce de Leon arrived . . . well, at least when Henry Flagler arrived.

I didn't even attempt to list the places to fish or play golf, or this book would have been much too heavy to carry around. It just goes without saying that there is plenty of both, because fishing and golf are why most people come to Florida to retire. And, you can do both all day, every day of the year.

The book includes some interesting tidbits about the state other than just its attractions. You'll find some history, some laws you ought to know, good places to eat, neat places to stay, and a lot of funny stories. I have also listed some further reference sources for special interest groups as canoeists, scuba divers, hikers; and other activities that Florida offers.

Please note that prices are omitted, because Florida rates are based on its high and low seasons. All over the state the seasons are different, and sometimes there is no high or low season at all. Your best bet is always to call first, and if you have time, call or write for a brochure. I also highly recommend advance reservations for overnight stays, no matter what time of year.

Florida's highways and byways are excellent and well marked. I have used the official state highway map for this book, because it is the map most visitors obtain. And, since Florida is really organized for tourists, you can acquire a brochure on just about any place in the state.

I thoroughly enjoyed the informality of Florida. A welcome smile awaited me no matter where I went. I really hated to finish this book, because Florida has so much to offer its permanent residents and numerous visitors. It's a way of life that is absolutely wonderful.

## MORE ABOUT FLORIDA

### General Information, Maps, and Events Calendar:

Florida Dept. of Commerce
Division of Tourism
Visitor Inquiry
126 West Van Buren St.
Tallahassee, FL 32399-2000
(904) 487-1462

### Fishing and Boating:

Game and Freshwater Fish Commission
620 S. Meridian St.
Tallahassee, FL 32399-1600
(904) 488-8347

## Golf:

Florida State Golf Association
P.O. Box 21177
Sarasota, FL 34238
(813) 921-5695

## State Parks:

Dept. of Natural Resources
Office of Communications
3900 Commonwealth Boulevard
Tallahassee, FL 32399-3000
(904) 487-2018

## Canoeing:

Florida Canoeing & Kayaking Assn., Inc.
P.O. Box 837
Tallahassee, FL 32302
(904) 422-1566

## Inns:

Association of Smaller and Historic Lodging
  Properties of Florida
9601 E. Bay Harbor Dr.
Bay Harbor Islands, FL 33154
(305) 868-4226

## Wineries:

Florida Grape Growers Assn.
P.O. Box 10766
Tampa, FL 33679-0766
(813) 254-4191

## Tennis:

Florida Tennis Assn.
801 N. E. 167th St., Suite 301
N. Miami Beach, FL 33162
(305) 652-2866

**Diving:**

Dept. of Commerce
Division of Tourism
Office of Sports Promotion
Collins Building, Suite 510 E.
Tallahassee, FL 32399-2000
(940) 488-9347

**Trails (bicycling, canoeing, hiking,
horseback riding, walking, and jogging):**

Division of Recreation and Parks
Dept. of Natural Resources
3900 Commonwealth Blvd.
Tallahassee, FL 32399
(904) 488-8243

---

Walt Disney World Resort
P.O. Box 10040
Lake Buena vista 32830-0040
(407) 924-4421

# HISTORY

About 6,000 years ago, give or take a few thousand, Florida assumed the shape of a giant thumb stretching out to the sea. Because of its southern location, this limestone peninsula escaped the ravages of the Ice Age, and its terrain remained flat and unscarred. Strange plants flourished in this warmer clime, and to escape the slowly marching glaciers, prehistoric animals migrated to Florida's paradise of food.

Florida became the home of huge, elephant-like mammoths, saber-toothed tigers, gigantic bears, tiny precursors of the horse and many other curious creatures, now extinct.

Today, beaches take up about 800 miles of Florida's coastline; 30,000 lakes dot the landscape; and underground springs create clear cool rivers and streams that are a source of enjoyment to divers and nature lovers. A Florida boast is that no place in the state is more than sixty miles from the ocean. By the year 2000 the state estimates its population will be eighteen million, plus another forty million or so tourists.

For a goodly number of people, the American Dream is to retire in Florida, and an amazing percentage achieve their goal. Florida has become the second fastest growing state in the nation with its warm skies, laid-back atmosphere, and a legislature that makes the state laws agreeable to the AARP members. Retirees can choose between a condo, a small Florida bungalow, a luxurious mansion, or even an RV park with all the amenities of a country club. And, because the state caters to retirees and tourists, you can find a golf course on practically every corner and a fishing spot on just about all the other corners.

This agreeable climate has been attracting man for at least 10,000 years, even before Florida attained its present geography. These "paleo-Indians" found a promised land on this lush peninsula with its semitropical forests and warm seas filled with fish and mollusks. Their fluted stones and flints have been discovered as far south as Warm Springs outside Venice about sixty feet underground.

By 5,000 B.C., civilization had advanced to primitive villages whose inhabitants were addicted to clams, oysters, and conchs. Discarded shells grew into huge garbage dumps euphemistically called "middens." However, the Florida natives were years ahead of the rest of North American Indians. Sometime about 2,000 B. C., these large, dark people created pottery, 800 years ahead of the tribes to the north. Agriculture followed, as did burial mounds and a highly developed civilization. Archaeologists race against progress to get to the Indian mounds before the developers and golf course builders bulldoze them into oblivion.

According to tradition, Florida was discovered by the Spanish conquistador, Ponce de Leon. However, it is quite possible that Giovanni Caboto (John Cabot) actually beat him to it. Cabot had already discovered Labrador after Columbus was blocked in his plans to reach China, and John and his son, Sebastian, sailed to the New World again in 1498 and reached the "Cape at the End of April." Cabot never landed here, but his maps indicate he discovered the Florida peninsula.

Be that as it may, Ponce de Leon sailed on Columbus's second voyage and established a "fort" of a sort on Puerto Rico. He was awarded the governorship of all Hispaniola, which wasn't very much at that date. But, Christopher's son,

Diego, wanted the title, and Ponce had to give in. As a consolation prize, King Ferdinand V told Ponce he could become governor of a fabled island called Bimini—if he could find it. Bimini was believed to have a fountain that flowed with the waters of eternal youth.

Ponce's early life is rather vague, but when he set forth for the fabled Bimini, he was about 53, a ripe old age in those days. So Ponce had a real incentive for discovering the fountain of youth. Another, better incentive was that he would practically own the lands he discovered and total mineral rights.

On April 2, 1513, (a month after embarking) Ponce landed somewhere between St. Augustine and the St. Johns River. As it was Easter season, *Pascua Florida*, The Feast of Flowers, Ponce named the land for the holiday, and it stuck.

From St. Augustine, Ponce sailed around the Keys and up the west coast. It was definitely more than some mythical island that the Spaniard had discovered. About where Fort Myers is today, Ponce landed and met the native Floridians. It was not a happy welcome by any means. In fact, the Indians were extremely hostile and shouted Spanish curse words at Ponce and his men. One belief is that the Florida Indians had been hunted as slaves by other discoverers. Another theory is that Indians from Puerto Rico and Haiti had escaped to Florida and warned them about the Spanish, and with good reason. More than one million Caribs had been killed or enslaved by the Europeans in less that eight years of occupation.

Ponce returned to Puerto Rico and sailed again in 1521 to Florida with the purpose of establishing a settlement and hopefully converting the natives to Catholicism. Putting ashore near Charlotte Harbor, the Spanish were attacked by a group of Calusas who refused to retreat. Ponce was struck by an arrow and although rescued by his men, he later died in Cuba. So much for the Fountain of Youth.

According to Catholic scholars, Ponce's priests were the first envoys of Catholicism to land in the United States.

A number of expeditions followed, and the Indians were as unfriendly as ever. More than 2,000 Spaniards lost their lives over Florida and its nonexistent gold.

The next ill-fated expedition came in 1528 when Tampa Bay sloshed over the feet of Panfilo de Narvaez. As with Coronado, the Indians told Narvaez that gold lay to the north.

Narvaez and his party left on foot for Apalachee with orders for his ships to meet him. Indian raids and mosquito attacks almost did Narvaez in, but he finally arrived at his Florida "El Dorado" to find, as did Coronado, absolutely nothing. In six small boats, the men sailed for Mexican shores. It was eight years later before Spain knew their fate when four survivors arrived in Mexico under the leadership of Alvar Nuñez Cabeza de Vaca who had a few grisly stories to tell about the cannibalistic Karankawa Indians of Texas.

Now it was time for the superman of conquistadors, Hernando de Soto, to make his assault on Florida. de Soto came ashore at Tampa Bay in May of 1539, and with him was a mighty show of force of 1,000 men. There to greet them was Juan Ortiz, a soldier with Narvaez who had been captured but managed to survive. Tortured by the Timucuan Indians, he was rescued from being roasted alive by the wife and daughters of the chief. Literally tearing him from the spit as he was being cooked, the women managed to save him. The Indian word for roasting Ortiz was *barbacoa,* so there you have the first American barbecue. Ortiz later escaped and wrote his terrible story. According to some historians, Ortiz' adventure was the basis for Captain John Smith creating his rescue by the beautiful Pocahontas.

Ruthlessly, de Soto and his fortune hunters hacked their way through the jungle and Indian villages looking for the gold and lavish cities of Mexico and Peru. They searched as far north as the Great Smoky Mountains, turned west, and after three years of frustration, de Soto died of fever on the Mississippi River. So far, the search for the Fountain of Youth had only met with the Fountain of Death.

Mainly what the gold seekers brought back to Spain were tales of incredible landscapes and savage Indians.

The wily French, noticing Spain's failures to settle Florida, took it upon themselves to build a fort near St. Augustine. This was too much for the arrogant Spanish. A huge armada arrived under Pedro Menendez de Aviles on the day of the Feast of St. Augustine, August 28, 1565. On September 8, Menendez formally broke ground for the first permanent settlement on American ground.

The French, under Jean Ribaut, planned to surprise the Spanish but a hurricane grounded their ships. Menendez captured the fort, killing all but the women and children. The conquistador had all but sixteen of the 150 Frenchmen slain, and Ribaut was beheaded. To this day, the site of this bloody slaughter is known as *Matanzas*, the place of slaughter.

St. Augustine was on shaky ground during an attack by Sir Francis Drake; hurricanes were always a threat, too, but the settlement always survived. And, with the establishment of Spanish rule, the end of the aboriginal Indians was a foregone conclusion. Those not killed or enslaved by the Spanish met their doom with measles and chicken pox. When England took possession of Florida in 1763, only about 200 aborigines were alive. Jesuit and Franciscan missionaries established about fifty missions, which the British later wiped off the face of the earth.

The aborigines were extinct, but the Indians were far from gone. Oconee Creeks from Georgia arrived in Florida to become the Seminoles.

To keep track of the different flags flying over Florida, you need a notebook handy. Britain began looking greedily at the small Spanish settlement of St. Augustine, so Spain built the impressive Castillo de San Marcos. However, battles were unnecessary. England managed to tack Florida on to its colonies with the First Treaty of Paris in 1763 by giving Cuba back to Spain. The Spanish vanished and the Creek tribes, who were friendly to the British, moved south.

The British created East Florida from the Atlantic to the Apalachicola River and West Florida from there to the Mississippi River. A wave of entirely new immigrants moved into the territories speaking English with harsh Cork and Cockney accents. These new settlers had no interest whatsoever in the revolutionary rumbling in the thirteen colonies to the north. You could almost say the American Revolution passed them by, except that Spain took advantage of England's plight with her colonies, and promptly captured all of West Florida. East Florida remained loyal to the British and even beat off American sorties against their boundaries.

So, in the Second Treaty of Paris in 1783, England gave Florida back to Spain after a brief twenty-year rule. But, the Spanish were as inept with their second acquisition of Florida as they were with the first. When Spain ceded their Louisiana territory to France and France sold it to the United States, it was inevitable that the United States would claim Florida as part of their new real estate.

Now, the British returned to help Spain, their ally in 1812, and sent troops to Pensacola. But, the struggling United States was not having any redcoats so close, even if Florida did belong to Spain. Andrew Jackson marched on Pensacola and routed the British out of Spanish Florida. The fact that he was trespassing didn't bother "Old Hickory" in the least.

The result was the First Seminole War of 1817-18. Andrew Jackson put down the affair by hanging a Seminole chief and also two British traders who he accused of inciting the Seminoles to war against the United States.

At last, Spain, sick of the affair and deeply in debt to the United States, exchanged Florida for $5 million in debts. In 1821, Andrew Jackson returned as the first American governor of Florida, a short stop on the road to the presidency.

The First Seminole War was an omen of bloodshed to come. Creeks had steadily migrated to Florida along with other Indians from Georgia and Alabama. They soon became known as "Seminolee" from a Creek word meaning "wild ones" or "runaways." Also steadily migrating to Florida were white Americans, and the pressure was on to move the Seminoles into a reservation in the west.

In 1823, thirty-two Indian chiefs agreed to a compromise and signed a treaty to move their tribes and black slaves to a reservation in central Florida. The United States would provide funds for a new life. As we might expect, neither side kept the treaty. Instead, in 1830, Congress signed a bill that all Indians must be sent west. This time, only seven chiefs signed the agreement. One young chief, destined for immortality, plunged his knife into the treaty and said, "The only treaty I will make is with this." Osceola became a Florida hero, and the Seminoles refused to leave for the west, or anywhere else. Major Francis Langhorne Dade and his men were massacred, and a seven-year bloodbath was begun.

The Seminoles managed to hold their own against the white man with their guerrilla warfare, but in 1837, the end came. It was not by superior tactics on the part of the United States generals, but by an act of treachery.

Osceola's great-grandfather was a Scot, but he preferred his Creek heritage. His rather strange name was a mixture of "asi," a sort of tea and "yaholo," the shout given by the Indians after a few sips of "asi." Osceola entered St. Augustine under a white flag of truce sent him by General Thomas S. Jessup. Jessup immediately arrested Osceola and threw him in prison along with his wives and children and other warriors. The great chief died a year later of malaria and went down in history as a Florida hero. The attending physician severed the Indian's head from his body and exhibited it in circus side shows.

With the capture and death of Osceola, the Seminoles were defeated. By 1842, 3,000 were shipped into the Oklahoma territory, even though some Seminoles escaped and hid deep in the Everglades under the leadership of Chief Billy Bowlegs. When they massacred some surveyors, the third and last Seminole War began. Bowlegs surrendered in 1858 and was sent west, but a small group was never captured and remained hidden in the swamps and sloughs of the Everglades.

Florida became a state in 1861, just in time to secede and join the Confederacy. Without time to recover from the Seminole Wars, the Civil War was devastating. Floridians fought bravely and well and stopped the Union advance at the Battle of Olustee in 1864, but all in vain. Ironically, the great abolitionist, Harriet Beecher Stowe, the author of *Uncle Tom's Cabin,* owned a cottage in Mandarin near Jacksonville.

Florida continued to be a wild frontier even after the nation was united again. In spite of the mosquitoes and all the diseases they carry, the sun and warm climate continued to lure settlers. Vincente Martinez Ybor came to Tampa in the 1880s, and his followers put Tampa on the map as the cigar capital of Florida. And, on the East Coast, a frostproof orange was developed by a Chinaman, Lue Gim Gong. But, it was the railroads that really brought civilization to the Florida swamps.

Beginning in 1885, Henry Morrison Flagler ran the tracks of the Florida East Coast Railroad from St. Augustine to a desolate beach that he christened Palm Beach. Next came Miami, then Homestead, and finally Key West in 1912. With opulent hotels along the rail line, the very rich decided Florida was the place to vacation—in the winter, of course, and at the Breakers Hotel or the Ormond or the Ponce de Leon Hotels. During this same era, the great entrepreneur, Henry Plant, constructed his railroad to Tampa and built the incredible Tampa Bay Hotel which is still in use today as a community college.

The Spanish American War was a boon to Florida, and Cuban rebels held forth in Tampa under Jose Marti, pleading the Cuban cause. Winston Churchill checked into the Tampa Bay Hotel to cover this ''little war,'' and Teddy Roosevelt organized his Rough Riders for their assault on San Juan Hill. After the ousting of Spain from the New World forever, the soldiers returned home with stories of the glitter and glamor of Florida. Entrepreneurs arrived in force, and by 1920 the Florida real estate boom was well underway.

Real estate salesmen found the gold that the Spanish missed. Thousands of acres of Florida swampland were sold and resold. Even the golden voice of William Jennings Bryan could be heard extolling the delights of living in exclusive Coral Gables. By the end of 1925, Miami Beach was lined with 481 hotels and apartment buildings. Architect Addison Mizner was designing grand and gaudy mansions in Palm Beach and Boca Raton. Money poured into Florida.

Doom and gloom were right behind this plethora of wealth, however. In 1926, a bitter winter hit Florida and then, to top off Mother Nature's nasty sense of humor, a devasta-

## Regions of Florida

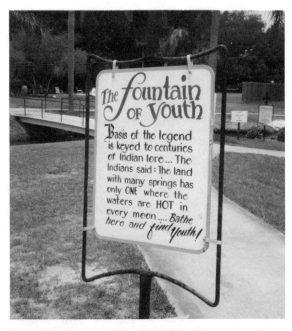

*Ponce de Leon never found the fabled Fountain of Youth
on the mythical island of Bimini, but he did discover a
mecca for vacationers and retirees.*

ting hurricane struck. Fortunes were being lost, but these
were a mere drop in the swamp compared to the crash of
the Great Depression. But, the Florida climate still drew
people eager for the sun.

After World War II, Florida began to recover. Miami Beach
built more hotel rooms than the other forty-seven states
combined. Pari-mutuel betting was legalized; Cape Canaveral began sending its missiles into the depths of space; Cuban
refugees began arriving by the thousands. But, the largest
impact on Florida's economy came in the form of a talking
mouse. Disney World created a bonanza for real estate
salesmen that was better than the old boom days of the 1920s.
Mickey is eternal and Disney World intends to keep him that
way. If ever a character discovered the Fountain of Youth,
it's Mickey Mouse.

# NORTHWEST FLORIDA

When the British acquired Florida in 1763, they divided it into West Florida and East Florida. West Florida was a huge chunk of real estate between the Apalachicola River and the Mississippi River. Its boundaries have shrunk to the Suwannee River on the east and the Alabama border on the west, but that's still a long haul on Interstate 10.

Most of the Florida Panhandle looks like it should be part of Georgia and Alabama: endless miles of pine trees and an antebellum atmosphere. However, just a few miles south of any point on Interstate 10 and you are dipping your toes in the whitest sand, bluest water, and most beautiful beaches in the world. And, from Pensacola to Fort Walton you can enjoy these beaches in some of the world's most luxurious resorts.

The western gateway to the Panhandle is the bustling city of Pensacola that has hoisted five flags in its Plaza Ferdinand VII. And, Pensacola wants the world to know that it was settled in 1559, six years before St. Augustine. But, the Spanish didn't like the hurricanes, the Indians, and the mosquitoes. After two years they abandoned their settlement, so St. Augustine received the title of Florida's oldest *continual* town. But, Pensacola does hold some sort of record with the fact that its government changed seventeen times in 300 years.

Tallahassee was founded in 1823 for no other reason than to be the capital of Florida. No one wanted to broach the southern peninsula with its jungles, and Pensacola and St. Augustine both wanted to be the capital. Finally, they compromised and chose a middle point and christened it with the Indian word for "old town" or "old fields." The new capital drew an interesting mix of characters, from rowdy backwoodsmen to royalty. Prince Achille Murat, nephew of Napoleon Bonaparte, married Catherine Willis, a great-grandniece of George Washington, in Tallahassee and they are buried in the Episcopal Cemetery. A big claim to fame for Tallahassee is that its Confederate troops fought so bravely at Natural Bridge that Tallahassee remained the only uncaptured rebel capital east of the Mississippi River.

Between cities you'll find Panhandle scenery a bit on the dull side. Pine trees and straight roads never take you over hill and dale. Florida is flat. And, interspersed among the whispering pines you will see a tremendous number of mobile homes, some in organized communities, and some just out there. But the Panhandle does have its charm, and you'll never regret finding its special places.

## TALLAHASSEE–APALACHICOLA–BLOUNTSTOWN

*SH 363 south to Woodville, 4 miles*

*Go 6 miles east to the Battle of Natural Bridge Monument*

*Backtrack to 363 and go south to SH 267, 5 miles*

*West on 267 to Wakulla Springs, 5 miles*

*SH 319 to US 98 and on to Panacea, 14 miles*

*Continue on US 98 to SH 370 to Alligator Point, 4 miles*

*Backtrack to US 98 to Carrabelle, 22 miles*

*Take 98 to Apalachicola, 22 miles*

*Take 98 to Port St. Joe, 22 miles*
*Take SH 71 to Wewahitchka, 24 miles*
*Continue 71 to Blountstown, 27 miles*
*Then SH 20 to Tallahassee, 43 miles*
*Total miles, 198*

ALTERNATE

*From Carrabelle, take a 45-minute ferry ride to Dog Island.*

ALTERNATE

*From Bristol on SH 20, take SH 12 to SH 271 to Torreya*
*State Park. Backtrack to SH 12 to I-10 to Tallahassee, 44*
*miles total.*

For Civil War buffs, the Battle of Natural Bridge Monument is a high point. When the Union forces invaded Florida towards the end of the war, they met a mishmash of regular Confederate troops, old men, and young boys. This ragtag army pushed the Yankees back, but it was a hollow victory. In a few weeks the war was over, and the Yankees returned to stay—forever. Florida was not into tourism in those bitter days and Floridians were extremely hostile to these new residents set on reaping the fruits of Reconstruction.

Just a few miles from the capital is Wakulla Springs, one of Florida's real treasures. Edward Ball was a political figure in the late 1900s and married into the wealthy DuPont family. Ball was soon worth $2 billion. He built a magnificent lodge next to Wakulla Springs, which the Indians called the "mysteries of strange water," because crystal clear water flows from an underground river at the rate of 600,000 gallons per minute.

In this gorgeous setting, Ball created a nature lover's paradise. Opening in 1937, The Lodge is filled with period furniture, and the decor of each guest room is unique. But, you can count on the modern conveniences of a private bath and air conditioning. Ball used the finest materials, from the Tennessee marble floors to the magnificent blue heron fireplace andirons. Now a state park, Wakulla Springs still retains its Old South hospitality. Call 904-224-5958.

Another part of Wakulla Springs' charm is a glass-bottomed boat ride that takes you far down the river to view the wildlife and lush vegetation. This trip is delightful, and you are told that the early Tarzan movies starring Johnny Weissmuller were filmed here. According to one guide, some of the monkeys used in these films escaped and their descendants still scamper about in the trees. If you don't spot the monkeys you will still see a myriad of Florida's beautiful birds, fish, turtles, deer, and the ever-popular alligators.

The setting is so primitive that the springs were also used for that epic motion picture from the 1950s, *The Creature from the Black Lagoon*. You can also swim in these cool waters, but you don't have to worry about any of the Creature's descendants rising from the "black lagoon."

An ideal stop for lunch is The Lodge's huge dining room. The atmosphere is wonderful, the food is good, the service excellent, and the prices reasonable.

A nice side trip is over to St. Marks. It's not much of a town, but one highlight is Posey's, "Home of the Topless Oyster." The mollusks are served raw with a sweet-and-sour

*Posey's is the "Home of the Topless Oyster," and a Florida landmark for good seafood.*

sauce on the side. Ramshackle and leaning to one side, Posey's has all the markings of a skid row waterfront bar. You can't wait to get inside and order up dozens of those "topless oysters." If Posey's is closed, nearby is the first Spanish outpost on the Florida coast, Fort San Marcos de Apalachee, now restored and open as a museum.

Posey's also has a restaurant in Panacea. The outside is not very imposing, however. In fact, it looks rather like a big metal building with no ambiance whatsoever. Look for the signs for Harbor House. It has good food and a great view of the Gulf.

Along this part of the Florida Coast you can forget condos, resorts, and manicured golf courses. People here fish to make a living, and the towns are just that, fishing villages.

Carrabelle is the embarkation point for the ultimate in splendid isolation—Dog Island. You even have to ask directions to locate the one and only ferry to take you over. Turn south on the road between the Burger Bar and the BP gas station. The fare is $8.50 each way, parking is free, and the trip takes about forty-five minutes. The schedule is extremely erratic, so you have to plan your trip very carefully. Reservations are a must, both on the ferry and at the Pelican Inn, 800-451-5294.

The pristine sands of Dog Island cover a beach about seven-and-a-half miles long. During World War II the island was a training base for the European Invasion, and that's the most activity Dog Island has ever seen or ever will see. The Nature Conservancy owns three-fourths of the island, and about 100 homes dot the remaining fourth. A few hearty souls like to live here year round, and a small dock and landing strip help them get to the mainland.

The amazing thing about Dog Island is no commercial establishments exist on the entire island. The Pelican Inn offers a meager eight apartments with everything furnished but food. That's right. You have to bring *all* of your food and drinks. The tap water is okay, but man does not live by tap water alone. Don't even think of telephones or TV, but the mail boat does chug in about three times a week.

The manager of the Pelican Inn will be waiting for you in his pickup truck when you arrive, so you don't have to haul the groceries down the sandy road. You won't get a key to your apartment because there are none. Only the nicest people come to Dog Island.

*The Pelican Inn on Dog Island offers the ultimate in splendid isolation.*

What is there to do on Dog Island? Not much. The inn has a hot tub, and if you desire an almost deserted beautiful beach, hiking, shelling, birdwatching, and strolling under soft dark skies by the light of a Florida moon, then you'll have a great time.

After Dog Island you may be ready for some city life, but you won't find it in Apalachicola. Even though Apalachicola is one of the best small towns in Florida, life is still on the quiet side. Like many names of Florida towns, Apalachicola is an Indian word with several translations. The best one is "friendly people," and it fits perfectly.

Dating back to 1831, Apalachicola began as a thriving port town, and its heyday was before the Civil War when cotton was king. Today, the seafood industry is its main source of income, and one of the world's largest oyster reefs is in Apalachicola Bay.

One of Apalachicola's citizens is definitely deserving of sainthood. Every time you sip a cool, iced drink, pay homage to Dr. John Gorrie. In 1851, this young physician was concerned for his patients ill with yellow fever. Desiring a method of cooling their rooms, he invented a machine which made ice, laying the groundwork for modern refrigeration and air conditioning. At the John Gorrie Museum you can see a replica of his original machine. Strangely enough, Dr. Gorrie was unable to sell his machine and died without seeing the far-reaching effects of his discovery.

For fun in the surf, the place to be is St. George Island State Park, with its nine miles of undeveloped beaches and dunes. A toll causeway from Apalachicola links the mainland with this barrier island, and you may drive your car on the beaches.

Located in the historic district of this delightful town is a completely restored and updated turn-of-the-century home that is now one of Florida's outstanding bed-and-breakfast inns. The Pink Camellia (904-653-2107) offers four guest rooms, each with a private bath, and a full breakfast that will last you most of the day. The house, with its comfortable wraparound porch, is furnished in contemporary appointments and artwork. Hosts Carole Jayne and Bill Barnes are both artists and also have a gallery downtown. Carole Jayne works mainly in enamels, and you won't be able to resist her earrings, nor her unique pens made with colorful postage stamps.

Across from the gallery is the old Gibson Inn which also takes guests and is famous for its fine dining.

Apalachicola boasts the state's oldest and largest marine event, the Florida Seafood Festival, which is held the first weekend in November. In addition to offering food and fun, the festival is a tribute to the Florida seafood industry. Apalachicola harvests 90 percent of the oysters and 53 percent of the shellfish in Florida.

On your way to Port St. Joe, don't miss Cape San Blas with its lonely little getaways. One of the best is the Old

*Apalachicola's historic Gibson Inn is filled with nostalgia, good food, and Florida hospitality.*

Saltworks Cabins (904-229-6097) which blend in so well with the natural surroundings you have to look closely for the entrance. The "saltworks" are remnants of Confederate salt works used during the Civil War when salt was all-important in the preserving of meat. The cabins are new and "squeaky" clean and very private. Take a canoe ride on the bay, play in Fort Crooked Tree, built by owners Don and Ardie Schreck for kids of all ages, and peek in the tiny museum and the craft shop with wares from local artists. But mostly, just enjoy the absolute peace and quiet. Nearby is St. Joseph's Peninsula State Park which boasts the least-crowded, most stunning beaches in Florida. You can watch the sun rise or set (or both) over crystal clear water on this narrow peninsula.

Port St. Joe was originally called Old St. Joseph, and it was quite a town with big hotels, two racetracks, and fine restaurants. It ranked commercially with the ports of Mobile, New Orleans, and its rival, Apalachicola. It was in St. Joseph that the delegates came to sign Florida's first constitution in 1839. This constitution became the law of Florida. Application for statehood was sent to Washington but ignored until Iowa came into the Union as a free state. Finally, on March 3, 1845, Florida was the twenty-seventh state admitted to the Union.

Today, Port St. Joe is the site of St. Joe Paper Company and also the third-largest chemical complex in Florida.

Heading north you pass through the small town of Wewahitchka (We-wa-hitch-ka), an Indian name that translates to "water eyes." The name comes from the two lakes in the heart of the city that appear to be a pair of eyes gazing into the clouds. Wewahitchka is an old lumber town, but fishermen love it. The Dead Lakes State Recreation Area has enough freshwater fishing to satisfy any rod and reel.

Just east of Blountstown, at Bristol, take an alternate drive to Torreya State Park. For biologists, Torreya State Park is a true Garden of Eden. Among the strange flora are pitcher plants that drown bugs and then eat them and the squat, fat, Torreya pine trees found no place else in the world. Only sturdy hikers are advised to take on the seven-and-a-half miles of trail. You go up and down bluffs and ravines and look over sheer 250-foot drops to the Apalachicola River.

One reason for the uncharacteristic vegetation is that the Apalachicola River carries seeds and seedling from the north. Plants that disappeared ages ago in the rest of the world thrive in Torreya, and the area is crammed with rare and endangered species. An out-of-print book by E. E. Callaway, a late Bristol resident, has a curious and rather delightful theory about the area. Since the woods are filled with such odd vegetation, Callaway concludes that this is the original Garden of Eden and Adam and Eve are buried in Liberty County. Are Cain and Abel nearby?

Also at Torreya, and open for tours, is the Gregory House from the 1850s, when cotton bales rather than rare seeds flowed down the Apalachicola River.

## TALLAHASSEE–HAVANA

*SH 157, 17 miles*

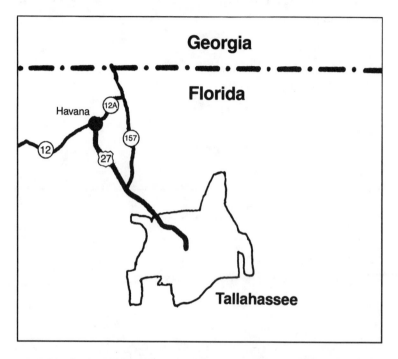

O.K., let's pronounce it right. It's Hay-van-a. This is the place for antique shopping. Havana has decided it would rather be an antique town than a ghost town, so you can prowl around at the H & H, an old red brick building with several antique shops, have a bite of lunch, and move on to the other shops.

## TALLAHASSEE–CEDAR KEY

*US 19-27 to Perry, 51 miles*
*US 19-98, south 4 miles*
*SH 361 to Steinhatchee, 40 miles*
*SH 51 to Tennille, 9 miles*

*US Alternate 27 to Old Town, 27 miles*
*US 19-98 to Chiefland (Manatee Springs), 9 miles*
*SH 345 or SH 24 to Cedar Key, 28 miles*
*Total miles, 168*

## ALTERNATE

*US 19-27 to Perry, 51 miles*
*US 27 to Mayo, 43 miles*
*US 27 to Branford, 15 miles*
*SH 349 to Old Town, 24 miles*
*SH 349 to Suwannee, 23 miles*
*Total miles, 156*

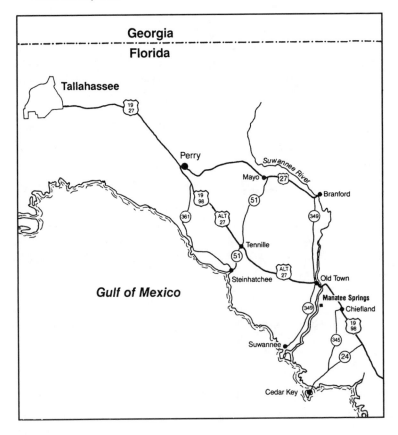

In 1965, Florida Governor Hayden Burns proclaimed Taylor County as the "Tree Capital of Florida," because more than 87 million pine seedlings were planted between 1928 and 1965. Perry, the county seat, celebrates the event with an annual Florida Forest Festival in the month of October. Just south of Perry is the Forest Capital State Museum. Inside are dioramas showing how the forest industry operated in the years before power chain saws, but don't miss the walk back to the Cracker Homestead behind the museum. Washtubs, lye soap, bare floors, swept yard, and a hard life were "the good old days" in those early pioneer years.

When General Zachary Taylor arrived in Steinhatchee during the Seminole War of 1835–42, he referred to the Isteenhatchee River where his post was located. Taylor went on to become the 12th President of the United States, but not much happened to Isteenhatchee except its name was shortened. It became a port of sorts for shipping cedar, but it never made the headlines in Florida real estate. Steinhatchee is part of the area some Floridians refer to as "the forgotten coast," which means it is lacking in condos and golf courses. You fish or eat fish, and that's just about all.

Roy's is everything you ever wanted in a good fish house—paper place mats, plastic dishes, plastic glasses, silverware wrapped in a paper napkin, condiment jars on the table, and divine seafood. But, if you must picnic and pass up all this backwoods fishhouse ambiance, ask for directions to Hagen's Cove.

Florida is famous for its clear bubbling springs. None may have the fame of Arkansas' Hot Springs or Yellowstone's sulphuric renderings, but for numbers, Florida bubbles over with 300 known springs. Folks who find springs fascinating are called "spring hoppers," and you'll hear them speaking in terms of "magnitude, flow, and MGD." "MGD" is easy as "Million Gallons Daily." And, a First Magnitude spring must discharge over six billion gallons daily, which is its "flow." Florida boasts twenty-seven First Magnitude springs and another seventy Second Magnitude springs at 6.46 MGD.

The reason for this incredible number of superstar springs is the Florida Aquifer of thick limestone. Enormous quantities of underground water flow throughout the state.

Just out of Chiefland on County Road 320 is one of the First Magnitude Springs with a MGD flow of 116.9, at Manatee Springs State Park (904-493-4288.) Secluded and absolutely lovely, here is Natural Florida at its best. A swamp boardwalk takes you over the Suwannee River on a great nature trail, but the best way to enjoy the springs is to paddle your own canoe. Rentals are available.

When you first see Cedar Key, you wonder if perhaps this was what Key West was like before the tourists found it. Yet, about a century ago this "mom-and-pop" town was one of the largest cities in the state. That was back in the days when kids wrote with cedar pencils rather than using calculators and ball point pens. The high tech age took over the pencils and a hurricane took over Cedar Key, and now you have a wonderful quiet little fishing town with a small art colony.

Another oddity about Cedar Key is that it is rather hilly, and in a state as flat as Florida, this adds to the town's charm. The architecture is anybody's guess, a museum coaxes you to remember the town was once "very important," and the creaky Island Hotel is more than 150 years old. Offshore islands sparkle with pristine beaches, and you have glorious choices among places to savor seafood by the sea.

Cedar Key stages a Seafood Festival in October that rates among the state's finest festivals. If it lives in the sea and it's edible, you'll slurp it down at Cedar Key. The Chamber of Commerce will send you the details (904-543-5600).

On down busy US 19-98 take SH 40 to another off-the-beaten-path little hamlet named Yankeetown. An old 1923 fishing lodge has been restored and houses a great restaurant called The Compleat Angler. Yep, the name of the lodge is the Izaak Walton. Units are rather rustic, but rates are budget.

## ALTERNATE

It's hard to believe in a state as overpopulated as Florida that there's a county with only one major town, but Lafayette County has a total population of less that 5,000 people. And, to add to the astonishing facts, the county is "dry" regarding alcoholic consumption. So much for attracting tourists in Lafayette County.

Yet, not far from Mayo on US 27 is Jim Hollis' Suwannee River Rendezvous (800-533-5276). The brochure gives a more glamorous picture than the actual facilities, but the resort does have appeal for families, divers, and campers. The restaurant is friendly and great for a snack if you don't want to cook. Because Lafayette is a dry county, you can't even bring your own booze on the grounds. Don't despair. The Huggy Bear Lounge has more than 200 kinds of beer and more than thirty varieties of wine coolers.

Otter Springs RV Resort (904-463-2696) is just west of Trenton on SH 26 and one of the oldest and largest private campgrounds in Florida. Choose the camping style that suits you best: hookups, furnished cabins, RV trailers for rent, or bring your own tent. Organized activities are available, and you can snorkel and scuba at Otter Springs. Snack at the canteen, but there is no lounge.

A popular getaway now is to head way down to the old port of Suwannee in the car, rent a houseboat and cruise back up for miles of uninterrupted scenic beauty on the famous Suwannee River. Miller's Marina & Campground (800-458-BOAT) offers luxurious, comfortable, maneuverable houseboats for couples or up to ten people. All you bring is your snorkel gear, fishing tackle, and food—lots of food because you won't find Kroger on the banks of this river. Stay a weekend, a week, or forever, way down upon the Suwannee River.

## TALLAHASSEE–WHITE SPRINGS (STEPHEN F. FOSTER MEMORIAL)

*US 90, Tallahassee to Monticello, 24 miles*

*US 90, Monticello to Madison, 32 miles*

*US 90, Madison to Suwannee River State Park, 20 miles*

*I-10, Suwannee River State Park to Live Oak, 15 miles*

*SH 136, Live Oak to White Springs, 12 miles*

*Total miles, 103*

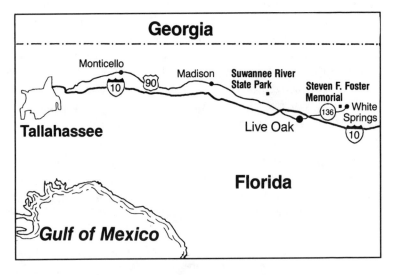

Known as the "Keystone County" of Florida, Jefferson is the only county that extends from Georgia on the north to the Gulf of Mexico on the south. Appropriately enough, the county seat was named for Thomas Jefferson's famous home, Monticello. But, before you pronounce it the way the Father of our Constitution would, get set to say "Mon-ti-sell-o," not "Mon-ti-chell-o." But, regardless, here at Monticello is a bastion of the Old South.

Monticello hoped to savor the booty of the tourist boom at the turn of the century, but its dreams never materialized.

And, it seemed the only sweetness in Jefferson County soil was turned into watermelons. In 1940, a reported 80 percent of the world's watermelon seeds were produced here. Impressive as that may sound, by 1960 the entire county could barely account for 8,500 souls.

Yet, Monticello is on the move, and now it's in the right direction. Historic preservation is a high priority, and the Monticello Opera House celebrated its 100th birthday in 1990 with a brilliant $900,000 restoration. Richard and Cheryl Lepanen have turned a 102-year-old home into a stunning bed and breakfast, Peppermill House (904-997-4600). Here is southern hospitality at it finest with lovely antique furnishings, a gigantic back yard filled with shade trees and a delicious breakfast to get the day underway. Try the Monticello Walking Tour and enjoy the romance of the Old South through the town's historic buildings and their stories.

A portion of the eastern boundary of Madison County is formed by the crooks and turns of the Suwannee River. Its county seat, also named Madison, is another of numerous pleasant small towns in northern Florida. Some accounts say both were named for President James Madison, and others say for Madison C. Livingston, who owned the land in 1838. The first American hero of World War II, Colin Kelly, lies in the Madison Oak Ridge Cemetery.

At the Suwannee River State Park, an overlook provides an impressive view of the confluence of the Suwannee and the Withlacoochee Rivers. Oak trees heavy with Spanish moss create a scenic setting for camping and picnicking.

And, Florida has one of those rare state songs that the entire country can join in: "Old Folks At Home." Suwannee is taken from an Indian word "sawani" which translates as "echo," and the refrain of "Old Folks At Home" does echo over the Stephen Foster State Folk Culture Center at White Springs loud and clear. A carillon tower with 93 bells rings out Foster's music on the hour and half hour.

Stephen Foster never saw Florida in his short and unhappy life, nor did he ever leave Pittsburgh to go "way down upon

*The carillon tower at the Stephen Foster State Folk Culture Center peals out "Old Folks At Home" and other beloved Foster melodies.*

the Suwannee River." He was often estranged from his wife and totally inept at managing his finances. He died in New York City at 37 with 38 cents in his pocket in 1863. Yet, "America's Troubadour" wrote more than 200 songs including "Oh! Susanna," "Camptown Races," "Jeanie With the Light Brown Hair," and "My Old Kentucky Home."

The Suwannee River rises in the Okefenokee Swamp of Georgia and meanders about 250 miles to the Gulf of Mexico. Foster picked the "S'wanee," as he spelled it, because it had a Southern sounding name. His alternate was the Peedee

River. Let's see, "Way down upon the Peedee River . . ." No. Peedee just doesn't have the ring to it.

Tenuous as Stephen Foster's ties are to Florida, White Springs is a charming spot. Early in the century, White Springs was a quite fashionable warm water spa and attracted the hero of San Juan Hill, Teddy Roosevelt, but now you are treated to a brief cultural education in Florida's ethnic groups. The Crackers, the Conchs, the Cubans, the Blacks, and the Seminoles are represented with dioramas depicting their contribution to Florida's history. One of the outstanding events here is the Florida Folk Festival, an annual gathering of folk musicians and craftspeople held on the Culture Center grounds in May.

In the Stephen Foster wing of the Culture Center are a piano on which the composer often played and a desk on which he arranged "Old Folks at Home." Florida designated Foster's song as the official state song in 1935.

## PENSACOLA–MILTON

*US 90, 21 miles*

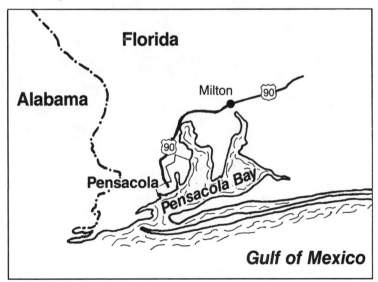

It's a temptation for newcomers to think of Milton as just another fast-growing town without much sense of the past. However, Milton's Historical District is on the National Register of Historical Places, and way back when the Blackwater River was a busy thoroughfare for four-masted schooners, Milton was quite an industrial town. Remnants still remain of those days, and a walking tour of the Historical District takes you "back when."

The 1914 Exchange Hotel has been restored by William S. Rosasco III as a bed and breakfast (904-626-1500). Rosasco also restored the 1912 Milton Opera House-Imogene Theatre.

Even though Milton is proud of its past, its officially designated title is now "Canoe Capital of Florida." Three pure, primitive river streams of the Blackwater, Sweetwater/Juniper and Coldwater Rivers make the Milton area a prime target for canoeists. The clear, spring-fed rivers flow at an average depth of two feet over soft, sandy bottoms with

*Florida's rivers are famous for great canoeing, and one of the best is the Blackwater River.*

sparkling white beaches lining the banks. Don't let that inky dark water fool you. It's actually crystal clear. Only the tannin from the cypress trees creates that "blackwater" effect. Just twelve miles north of Milton on SH 87 is Adventures Unlimited (904-623-6197) at Tomahawk Landing. Your choice is a lazy canoe trip anywhere from four to seventeen miles a day, tubing on the Coldwater River, picnicking, camping, or renting one of the furnished cabins. Remember, the cabins have wonderful screened porches when the buzz-bombers come out at night, and fireplaces for winter evenings.

## PANAMA CITY–DEFUNIAK SPRINGS–MARIANNA

*US 98 (County Road 30-A), Panama City to Seaside, 37 miles*

*US 331, Seaside to DeFuniak Springs, 25 miles*

*US 331, DeFuniak Springs to Highest Point in Florida (near Lakewood), 27 miles*

*County Road 2A to SH 2 to Graceville, 44 miles*

*SH 77, Graceville to Chipley, 14 miles*

*SH 77, Chipley to Falling Waters, 5 miles*

*Continue on SH 77 to Panama City, 37 miles*

*Total Miles, 189*

ALTERNATE

*SH 2, Graceville to Malone, 16 miles*

*SH 71, Malone to Greenwood, 7 miles*

*SH 69, Greenwood to Grand Ridge, 15 miles*

*US 90, Grand Ridge to Marianna, 13 miles*

*Total Miles, 51*

All of Panama City's brochures invite you to enjoy "The World's Most Beautiful Beaches," and there's no doubt that the grass-green water and stark white beaches are the most outstanding feature of this area. This unique sand was born thousands of years ago as quartz crystals in the Appalachian Mountains. Over the billions of years, these crystals have

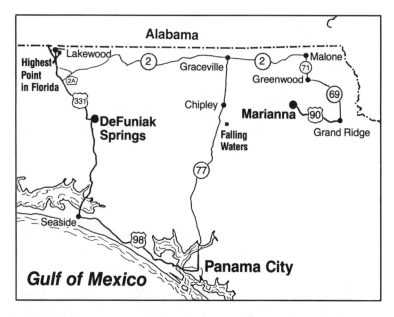

been broken down, washed, bleached, ground and polished, and then deposited along 27 miles of the North Florida coastline. Resorts, motels, condos, attractions for all ages, and unlimited restaurants are the order of the day at Panama Beach. For more information, call 800-PCBEACH.

The biggest resort news in Florida is the new town of Seaside. Florida's beaches are usually littered with concrete high-rises, but at Seaside, houses and cottages stand alone amid their naturally landscaped yards, separated by New England white picket fences. No two houses are alike, and some may be three stories high, but only one room wide. Victorian gingerbread rubs shoulders with Japanese avant-garde. And, each little "townsite" has its own beach pavilion. Sitting high atop the dunes, all these pavilions are brilliant silhouettes, white against the blue of the sky and the sea. Restrooms and showers are provided at the foot of each pavilion.

Perhaps the ultimate rental at Seaside is one of the Honeymoon Cottages. Six charming two-room houses have been crafted to offer down-filled furniture, fireplaces, steam baths, whirlpools, thick terry robes, and even room service to bring in the caviar and champagne.

Seaside is more than just a collection of vacation homes. A commercial building, Dreamland Heights, includes a gourmet food market and deli. Upstairs are eight cabins: five "Boisterous" cabins face the sunset, and three others poetically named The Mathematician, The Musician, and The Tragic Poet face the sunrise. Across the highway on the beach is a delightful assortment of shops built on the open-air concept of a Mediterranean street market.

*The quaint village of Seaside is reminiscent of New England with its charming Victorian homes and picket fences.*

Nothing like Seaside exists anyplace else in Florida. Not only is Seaside the ultimate in beach vacations, it is also the ultimate in "seaside quaint." Summer is the high season for rates at Seaside, but every season is wonderful. For that perfect getaway, call 800-653-0296.

Near Seaside is a place of tranquility and serenity entirely different from the beachfront resorts. The site of Eden State Gardens was once the hub of the rich Wesley Lumber Company. The mansion was built in 1897, and William Henry Wesley and his descendants lived in it until 1953. Even after the mill and the company houses disappeared, the Wesleys remained. Finally, even the Wesleys disappeared, and the home was purchased and restored by Miss Lois Maxon. In 1968, Miss Maxon donated the house and grounds to the state of Florida in memory of her parents. A plaque with a quote by Amos Bronson Alcott reminds you, "Who loves a garden, still his Eden keeps."

Many guests at the Beaches of South Walton feel they have found Shangri-la and can't be dragged away, but for those with a more adventurous spirit, there is life north of the beaches. DeFuniak Springs is filled with grand old homes built in the late 1800s. Most belonged to visitors who came for the winter sessions of Chautauqua. These sessions took the form of concerts, symposiums, plays, lectures, and Bible study. Begun around Lake Chautauqua in New York, this educational and cultural movement migrated over eastern and central parts of the country. DeFuniak Springs' Chautauqua building still stands, and book lovers will appreciate that the town has the oldest continuously-operating library in its original building in the United States. The Walton County Chamber of Commerce (904-892-3191) will be glad to send you information.

At the intersection of I-10 and SH 331 is DeFuniak Springs' newest industry, the Chautauqua Winery. You are welcome to come in for a visit to the tasting room, sip a glass of Chautauqua wine, tour the shining stainless steel vats, and stroll through a small vineyard. It will probably be a long time before you associate Florida with wine as you do with orange juice, but several wineries are in operation across the state.

If you ever had any doubt about Florida's low elevation, just before you get to the Georgia border you'll hit the high spot in the state. A small marker proclaims the highest point in Florida to be a whopping 345 feet.

A backroads ride over to Graceville and Malone is pleasant with tall pines and wildflowers. Don't miss the 1860 antebellum home, "Great Oaks," just out of Greenwood. It's not open to the public, but it is impressive to photograph.

*Sportswear shops will never carry ski clothes in Florida!*

Many of Florida's rivers and towns are loaded with Indian names which is definitely not unusual anywhere in the United States. But, if you are wondering how Two Egg, Florida, got its name, stop at Lawrence's grocery for a cold drink and chat with owner Nell King. She'll give you the following explanations, and you can choose the one you like:

The first sale at the old country store was for two eggs.

A load of eggs was being delivered and all but two were broken on arrival.

A little boy used to swap two eggs for candy.

Or you can make up your own, but don't miss the country store. It's just a few feet off SH 69 on County Road 69A. You can even get a T-shirt or hat with Two Egg, Florida, on the front.

The obelisk in the center of downtown Marianna stands in memory of the "Cradle to Grave" Militia that gallantly defended Marianna in 1864 from a Union raid under General

*Several good stories from Nell King at the Lawrence Grocery will tell you how Two Egg got its name.*

Asboth. Old men and small boys came to defend their town, but nearly sixty were casualties. Ironically, Marianna was known for its staunch Union sentiment. The battlefield site is east of town on US 90. Just west of Marianna is the Florida Caverns State Park, the site of the only publicly accessible limestone caverns and underground caves in Florida. It's not Carlsbad Caverns, but the stalactites and stalagmites are breathtaking. Florida has a plethora of limestone caverns, but for most of them you have to don your scuba gear to enjoy their beauty.

Nearby at Chipley is Falling Waters State Recreation Area, another limestone phenomenon. Falling Waters Sink is a cylindrical, smooth-walled pit, 100 feet deep and 15 feet in diameter. Water flows into the sink to an underground cavern at the bottom. The setting is heavily forested, and an overlook platform provides an excellent view, but don't look up to see a waterfall, look down. Other sinks in the area may be seen from a boardwalk. Falling Waters Park is also the site of the first attempt to drill an oil well in Florida.

REGION 2

# NORTHEAST FLORIDA

The largest city in the United States is not New York, but Jacksonville, Florida, in land area, anyway. Encompassing 841 square miles, the city spans both banks of the St. Johns River. Sort of overlooked by the tourist crowd, Jacksonville still has one of the South's finest zoos, one of its busiest ports, and one of the world's largest and tallest objects, spraying water up to 120 feet in the air: the Friendship Fountain. Affectionately called "Jax," the city was named after the first military governor of Florida as a Union State, Andrew Jackson.

On May Day in 1562 French Admiral Jean Ribaud discovered a break in the land of an unexplored coast of Florida. The adept Frenchman promptly named it the River of May. Three years later when Don Pedro Menendez de Aviles defeated Ribaud's troops, he rechristened the river the River of San Mateo. About 1610 the river's name changed again, to San Juan del Puerto after a mission on St. Georges Island. When the British took over Florida in 1670, San Juan was

38

anglicized to St. Johns. No matter what the name, the St. Johns River has played an important role in Florida history. If you are ever on a TV game show, and the question comes up, "What is the only river in North America that flows north?" you can win the prize with, "The St. Johns in Florida." When one old-timer was asked where the St. Johns begins, he answered, "Oh, down thataway a piece, somewhere beyond hell and blazes." Accordingly, one of the southernmost lakes on the St. Johns chain is called "Lake Hellen Blazes." For more than 300 miles the St. Johns waters are a paradise for river explorers. Hundreds of side streams are full of discoveries, and along their shores is truly the "natural Florida." The St. Johns poses a real adventure in northeast Florida, and nautical charts detail everything of interest along the way.

While Jax may be the largest city in the United States, no one seriously contests that Florida also has the oldest city in the United States, St. Augustine. Here is what St. Augustine has to say about its claim: St. Augustine was the first permanent settlement by Europeans in what is now the continental US, 42 years before Jamestown. And to make sure that Pensacola doesn't make any waves about actually being older, St. Augustine adds, the oldest *continuous* settlement. And, another fact, no trip to Florida is complete without a sip of that bad-tasting water from the Fountain of Youth attraction that Ponce de Leon never found.

Gainesville, home of the University of Florida, was once named Hog Town, but is now called Gator Town for its football team.

Alachua County is proud of its historic little towns, and the Historical Commission has published a set of driving tours. Few of the homes on the tours are open to the public, but they are interesting to read about and see. You will also enjoy the William Bartram Trail in Alachua County, a car and bicycle self-guided tour (904-374-5210).

## JACKSONVILLE–AMELIA ISLAND

*SH A1A Jacksonville to Amelia Island, 29 miles*

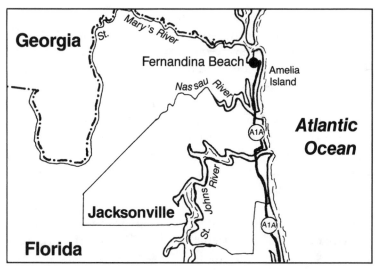

Just on the rim of the Georgia border you will find Florida's "Golden Isle," Amelia Island. This lovely island with the lovely name was christened in honor of the unmarried daughter of King George II of England. Here you will find the only location in the United States to have eight flags fly in its ocean breezes. In addition to the big powers of Spain, France, England, the Confederacy, and the United States, there were the "Patriots of Amelia Island" in 1812, the Green Cross of Florida in 1817, and the Mexican Rebel Flag in 1817.

The golden years from 1875–1900 saw business at its height of prosperity. Tourists, shipping, and the Spanish-American War created Fernandina Beach's Historic District which is still doing business today and retains a charm unlike any other part of the vast Florida coastline.

Park your car and head for the waterfront. You'll find Old Dobbin hitched to a carriage ready to take you for a ride around town. Over the clip-clop of Dobbin's hooves, your driver will give you a historic rundown on Fernandina Beach.

Sometimes a fort tour can be a ho-hum visit and you have to be a real fort fan to enjoy its story. But, Fort Clinch takes you on a trip back to 1864 in a most unusual way—by candlelight. A "soldier" who is actually a member of the Florida Park Service guides you through the fort by flickering candles that softly glow against the masonry walls. Although originally a Confederate fort, it was retaken by Federal troops in 1862, so your guide will entice the men to enlist in the Union Army and the women to sign on to help out in the laundry.

Fernandina Beach is a casual town with a real laid-back ambiance. You really don't need reservations at the many fine restaurants and prices are reasonable. The old Palace Saloon will draw you like a magnet. For a romantic drink, you can't pick a more colorful spot with its massive hand-carved mahogany bar, pressed tin ceiling, and gigantic murals dating back to 1907.

Shops and galleries line the streets with names like Faith Wick's World of Little People (a renowned doll maker), and the Three Star Saloon (actually a gift boutique), and the Eight Flags Antique Gallery. Everywhere you look you'll see a plaque designating Fernandina's buildings on the National Register of Historic Places, particularly along Centre Street where you'll find most of the shops.

On South Third is Florida House which may well be Florida's oldest tourist hotel. Cuban patriot Jose Marti and U. S. President Ulysses S. Grant are said to have lodged at the Florida House. Recently renovated, the Florida House is now open as a bed and breakfast (904-261-3300). Also on South Third is the San Carlos Winery offering tours and tasting.

If you love the roar of an unsettled surf to lull you to sleep, just a short drive down SH A1A takes you to The 1735 House. If you didn't know better, you would think you had just come upon the seashore of Cape Cod. This wonderful white clapboard inn with its picket fence is the only country inn in Florida that directly faces the Atlantic Ocean, and a white sand beach is right at your doorstep.

The 1735 House (904-261-5878) was actually built in the 1920s and got its name from the year that Georgia Governor James Oglethorpe explored Amelia Island. Inside are five suites with nautical decor, and even though each has a tiny kitchenette, the housekeeper arrives each morning with a wicker basket filled with a savory continental breakfast.

Perhaps you've always yearned to spend a night in a lighthouse. Just a short walk from The 1735 House is a little four-story lighthouse that sleeps six and can be rented by calling the inn.

If a resort is more your style, Amelia Island is the home of the world famous Amelia Island Plantation. Golf, tennis, dancing, dining, spa, beach, swimming pool . . . the activities go on and on. Special packages are available (800-342-6841).

## JACKSONVILLE–ST. AUGUSTINE AND MARINELAND

*SH A1A to St. Augustine, 30 miles*

*SH A1A, St. Augustine to Marineland, 17 miles*

*Total miles, 47*

Once upon a time, many many years ago, you could drive down SH A1A from Jacksonville to Palm Beach and enjoy endless miles of empty beaches, funky tourist spots, some mom-and-pop motels, and tacky seafood eateries. All that was before Cape Canaveral, condos, RV parks, golf clubs, resorts, and developers interested in a fast buck. If you even catch a fleeting glimpse of the Atlantic Ocean as you drive this frantic highway these days, you're lucky. About the only spot left of ''Old Florida'' on SH A1A is St. Augustine, and even it is beginning to look new around the edges.

The favorite word in St. Augustine is ''oldest.'' You'll visit the Oldest Store Museum, the Oldest Wooden Schoolhouse, the Old Jail, and the Oldest House . . . all in America's oldest town. But, you certainly don't want to be the oldest tourist

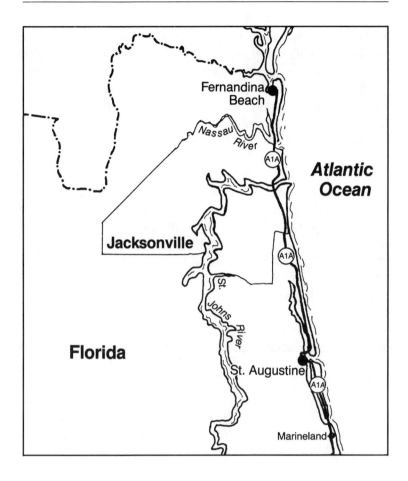

in St. Augustine, so start your tour with The Fountain of Youth. We all know that Ponce de Leon never found it, but now huge billboards make its location hard to miss.

After a sip of the sulfide elixir of the Fountain of Youth, stroll around the grounds, and pose for a picture next to the statue of Ponce de Leon, and visit the other attractions in the park. It's all very touristy, but great fun.

Dominating St. Augustine is the impressive Castillo de San Marcos, the oldest masonry fort in the continental United States. Construction was begun in 1672 under Spain, and finally the bombproof rooms and 14-foot-thick walls were finished in 1695. Coquina, a locally quarried shell-rock, was used to build the fort and artillery shells were "swallowed" by the coquina causing little damage. However, the fort was built somewhat too late, as Sir Francis Drake pillaged the town in 1586 and then the English pirates plundered again in 1668.

Walk the narrow streets around the Oldest House, and you'll capture the flavor of the town in its original form. Down on the bayfront a 208-foot stainless steel cross has been erected where Don Pedro Menendez is said to have first walked ashore. Located in the historic district is the charming Kenwood Inn. If you enjoy staying in a bed and breakfast, try The Kenwood Inn (904-824-2116) or the Casa de Solana. Casa de Solana (circa 1763) is a renovated colonial home with four suites and full breakfast (904-824-3555).

Henry M. Flagler, a modern day patron saint of St. Augustine, built the magnificent Ponce de Leon Hotel and the Alcazar Hotel. Flagler, the railroad tycoon, would be pleased to see them still in existence today. The Alcazar is now the Lightner Museum, and the Ponce de Leon is now a college. What better spot for lunch than the Cafe Alcazar? This used to be the indoor pool of the hotel, but now in keeping with the grandeur of the past, tables are set with fresh flowers, linen tablecloths, and china. At the top of the menu, take note of the good advice, "We have served more than 2,800 specials. None of them have ever been the same. If you miss the one today, you will never get a chance to order it again." For a special evening of dining, try the Columbia Restaurant in the heart of the Historic District. The food is just as magnificent as the original restaurant in Tampa established in 1905. If you want dinner in your own private thatched hut overlooking the bay at sunset, the place is Capt. Jim's Conch House. Antique lovers will admire the collection of nautical relics used throughout the restaurant, and the palm frond roof is the work of the Ponce brothers who own the Conch House and a Seminole Indian and his son. If the private huts are occupied, you can still dine on the outdoor deck or inside the Conch House. As expected, seafood and conch are the main items on the menu.

St. Augustine has an abundance of other tourist attractions, however, many of them are not on the historic list. But, you won't run out of things to do and see. For a vacation packet, contact the St. Augustine Chamber of Commerce (904-829-5681).

## MARINELAND

In the early 1930s three men searched for a remote section of the northern Florida coast to build the world's first underwater motion picture studios. A new word was coined to describe their project—oceanarium. Their goal was to build a place where various species of marine life lived together as they do in the sea. These three men were W. Douglas Burden, a great-great-grandson of Commodore Cornelius Vanderbilt; Cornelius Vanderbilt Whitney, chairman of Pan American Airways and producer of *Gone With The Wind;* and Count Illia Tolstoy, grandson of the Russian novelist Leo Tolstoy. The result of their endeavor opened in 1938 as Marine Studios.

As traffic whizzes up and down SH A1A, it is difficult to visualize this as a once-uninhabited Florida beach. But Marineland, as Marine Studios later became, developed into Florida's premier attraction overnight. During World War II, Marineland was a training arena for combat dogs and an experimental area for shark repellant research. It was after great expense that Marineland reopened in 1946 to once again become a world famous attraction.

Adolph Frohm, a Ringling Brothers Circus animal trainer, was hired in 1949 to begin unprecedented experimental efforts to train dolphins. His A-plus student was Flippy, a two-year-old dolphin that became the world's first "educated dolphin." Flippy was star quality and drew huge crowds to a special stadium built just for his talents.

*Since 1938, dolphins have frolicked at Marineland, the world's first oceanarium.* Photo courtesy of Marineland.

Dolphins are still the stars at Marineland, but visitors forget that much of what we know about dolphins results from the research conducted at this park. No wonder that Marineland has received the honor of being placed on the National Register of Historic Places.

Plan to spend a full day at this historic park. Visit lovely Whitney Park landscaped with indigenous plant life. See the full-size replica of the jaws and teeth of a giant prehistoric shark estimated to have been about 70 feet long. Talk about ''Jaws!'' This critter's mouth opens to five feet tall. Penguins, sea lions, sharks, dolphins, and thousands more marine specimens are part of the wonders of Marineland (904-471-1111).

Marineland spans both sides of SH A1A. Don't miss either side. A program gives times of the dolphin shows, the sea lion training, and penguin feedings. The Herrick Shell Museum has more than 6,000 fabulous shells, and "Wonders of the Spring" is the world's largest freshwater exhibit.

Right across the road from Marineland is a luxurious Quality Inn with oceanfront rooms (800-228-5151). Make this mini-resort your headquarters while exploring the Northeast Florida Coast.

## JACKSONVILLE–PALATKA (St. Johns River Drive)

*SH 13/207 to Palatka, 63 miles*
*US 17, Palatka to Jacksonville, 31 miles*
*Total miles, 94*

As you leave Jax to begin your drive down the historic St. Johns River, pause for a moment at the tiny town of Mandarin, named for the Mandarin orange. In 1867, the famous author of *Uncle Tom's Cabin* purchased a cottage here. For 17 winters, Harriet Beecher Stowe welcomed tourists arriving on the steamer *Mary Draper*, and for 75 cents each, passengers were allowed to admire her and her domain. Her book *Palmetto Leaves* (which did not outsell her first novel) did inspire winter visits to the St. Johns valley by rich and fashionable tourists. A small chapel is dedicated to Harriet Beecher Stowe in Mandarin.

If you turn west off SH 13 onto Mandarin Road, you'll find the heart and soul of the "old town." Mandarin Road leaves the highway and arches along the river, and then returns to the main highway several miles south. Watch for the stone marker with the words "Store Lane" (no longer a lane). However, many years ago a lane went down to the river where there were the original general store and post office near the docks. From these docks, hundreds of barrels of mandarin oranges were shipped all over the world.

As you drive along Mandarin Road, you will see old homes built around the time of the Civil War. The church that Mr. and Mrs. Stowe helped build was destroyed during

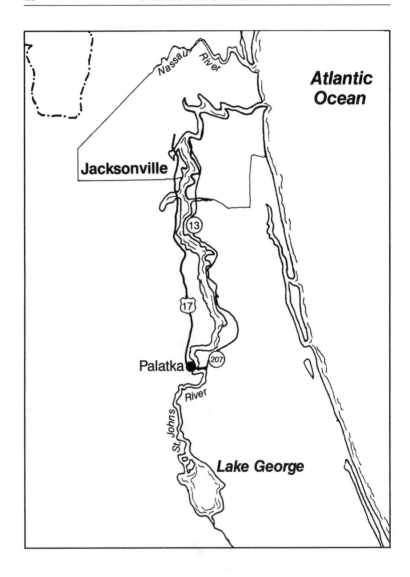

Hurricane Dora, but the new church is on the original site purchased in 1883 for $121.75. The Stowe house is gone. Their son Charles believed his parents had been mistreated in Florida and he had their home torn down to erase all evidence of their ever having lived in Mandarin.

Switzerland, once known as New Switzerland, was the site of the impressive Fatio Plantation. Across the river at Hibernia stood the beautiful Fleming Plantation, and the story of the actual people who lived through the 1800s at these homes is told in Eugenia Price's novel, *Margaret's Story*. It was near Picolata that William Bartram, son of a famous English botanist, settled in 1766. In England, William lived off his father's largess while he wrote poetry about his unrequited love for his cousin Mary. No one seems to have read his poems, including cousin Mary. Later, he was commissioned by England to travel the Carolinas, Georgia, and Florida to collect rare plants and seeds and to draw birds, reptiles, insects, and native plants. The result was a book that made Billy Bartram a famous scientist. Don't worry about the book's title, the reading is only for the dedicated Bartram fans, and you can bet cousin Mary never parted its covers. Signposts throughout the southeast commemorate the William Bartram Trail.

Tocoi was the terminus of the St. Johns Railway which in the 1870s conveyed freight and steamship passengers to St. Augustine over 18 miles of wooden track.

Hastings originated as a result of the elegant Ponce de Leon Hotel in St. Augustine. Henry Flagler, the owner of the hotel, wanted fresh vegetables to be readily accessible for the meals of his wealthy guests. He persuaded his cousin, Thomas Horace Hastings, to develop a farm nearby. In 1890, Hastings established his Prairie Garden Plantation on a 1,589-acre site where he experimented with cauliflower, cabbage, and Bermuda onions. A community evolved and eventually grew into a bustling farming center now called The Potato Capital of Florida.

A major steamboat landing in the late 1800s, Palatka was famous for its elegant hotels. The Putnam House inaugurated its 1879 season with a grand ball in honor of General Grant. Palatka has renovated its river district, and Riverfront Walk and Park combines pathways, cool breezes, and pleasure boating.

*On SH 204 east of Hastings, watch for a yard filled with fiberglass animals.*

In Palatka, watch for signs to Ravine Gardens. Giant sinkholes created three ravines that have been transformed into gorgeous gardens. You can drive the three-mile rim and enjoy the terraces, suspension bridges, miniature waterfalls, and rock formations, or you can hike the many paths leading to the floor of the sinks. An incredible 100,000 azaleas have been planted so you may want to enjoy the beauty of Ravine Gardens in March and April.

Several years ago the Palatka area boasted its own down-home monster. In tiny Bardin, northwest of Palatka, residents liked to talk about a hairy half-ape, half-man creature about seven feet tall that stalked the woods. No one seems terrified of the yeti-type apparition and they speak rather kindly of "Booger."

The drive back to Jax isn't as interesting as the way down. Green Cove Springs stores boats of all sizes that have been confiscated by U. S. Customs. The town was a major steamboat landing in the late 1800s, and its Clarendon Hotel hosted winter vacationers in unsurpassed elegance.

The Clarendon is gone, but for old Florida charm, try The Club Continental, a Mediterranean-style inn overlooking the St. Johns River in Orange Park (904-264-6070). The Club, built in 1923 as the Palmolive family estate, now hosts seven riverview suites with lush gardens, seven tennis courts, three pools, and a pre-Civil War Riverhouse Pub.

## GAINESVILLE–RAWLINGS HOME–
## MICANOPY–MCINTOSH

*SH 20 east of Gainesville to County Road 325, 8 miles*

*County Road 325 to Cross Creek, 13 miles*

*County Road 346 to Micanopy, 8 miles*

*US 441 to McIntosh, 7 miles*

*US 441 to Gainesville, 19 miles*

*Total miles, 54*

The Pulitzer Prize for fiction was awarded in 1939 to Marjorie Kinnan Rawlings for her novel *The Yearling*. Rawlings was a New York society girl who gave up the city life for a cracker house in Cross Creek, Florida. In *The Yearling* she captured the poignancy of a boy's coming of age in the scrub country around Cross Creek. It became a major motion picture starring Gregory Peck and Claude Jarman, Jr. Rawlings went on to write other novels, but none achieved the acclaim of *The Yearling*.

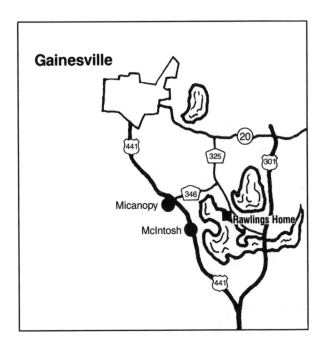

The cracker house where she lived and wrote appears much as it did when the author made it her home. Additions to the main structure, plus indoor plumbing, a carport, and a screened porch created the atmosphere that Rawlings wanted. After her success, famous authors came to call and spent days at the Cross Creek home. Actor Gregory Peck was also on her list of guests. This was not a hideaway for the author at all. This was a working farm and Rawlings did her best to make it a paying venture. It was a constant struggle to keep the citrus grove producing and during the fifties a frost killed the trees.

Marjorie Rawlings married Norton Baskin in 1941 and divided her time between St. Augustine and Cross Creek. She died in 1953 at age 57.

The author's will stated that she wanted her home to remain a home, not a museum. Tours are conducted in small groups and no rooms are roped off. You are welcome to touch her furniture and belongings. The kitchen will be warm with a batch of cookies in the stove, and your guide will tell you many details of this brilliant writer's fascinating life here at Cross Creek.

The tiny hamlet of Micanopy (Mick-a-no-py) was named for a Seminole chief whose only claim to fame was he agreed to give up his lands to the white men during the second Seminole War. Micanopy is the oldest inland town in Florida and was occupied by the Timucuan Indians before the Seminoles. When William Bartram arrived in 1774, the settlement was called Cuscowilla and the chief was named Ahaya but called Cowkeeper by the English. When William Bartram visited this area, he was given the name "Puc Puggy," or "flower hunter" by Cowkeeper. Following Ahaya's rule were King Payne and finally Chief Micanope. The Micanopy Historic District, which is practically the entire town, was placed on the National Register of Historic Places in 1983.

Micanopy is one of those rare towns in Florida caught in a time warp. Nothing appears to have changed since the mid-1800s, and you are overwhelmed with its charm. Wonderful old buildings and homes line the few streets, antique shops offer delightful browsing, and the 1875 Herlong Mansion is now a bed and breakfast (904-466-3322).

As you stroll the quiet streets with their giant live oaks casting a canopy of shade, you'll be so glad you found this quiet elegance in a state otherwise devoted to golf courses and condos.

Another town just down the road from Micanopy has been caught in a time warp, too. Turn off US 441 and meander down the wide peaceful streets of McIntosh. Baskets of flowers hang from the old lampposts, wide lawns stretch back from the sidewalks, and majestic Victorian homes tell a story of a bygone era. "Merrily," built in 1888, is now a bed and breakfast (904-591-1150).

You won't find excitement in McIntosh, nor will you find numerous shops or restaurants. You will find a wonderful serenity and peace of mind that is rare, indeed.

*Micanopy is a taste of the Old South with magnolias, moss, and antique shops.*

On your return, just a little over a mile north of Micanopy is the entrance to Payne's Prairie State Preserve. This low basin was formed by settlement when the underlying limestone dissolved, and is now covered by marsh and wet prairie vegetation with areas of open water.

Among the most significant natural and historic areas of Florida, Payne's Prairie was the center of man's activities for many centuries. Prehistoric Indian artifacts have been found, and in the 1600s it was a large Spanish cattle ranch. It was described in detail by William Bartram who visited the "Alachua Savanah" in 1774. Most of the animals which Bartram described so long ago still abound on the prairie. The preserve offers all park recreation facilities, a Visitor Center, and an observation tower.

# CENTRAL WEST FLORIDA

Slick-tongued promoters have conjured up names for just about every inch of Florida's beaches (Gold Coast, Treasure Coast, etc.), but the best they have come up with for the chunk of land in Central West Florida is Pinellas Suncoast. Pinellas is the name of the county that includes St. Petersburg and Clearwater.

Developers have moved in and appear determined to block out all views of the Gulf with resorts, retirement farms, and shopping centers. So, from New Port Richey to Fort Myers, life moves in the fast lane. Tampa Bay is totally polluted and its docks have made Tampa one of the top ten ports in the country. Sarasota used to be famous just for its Ringling Museum, but now caters to the very affluent with exclusive resorts and the fashionable shopping district, St. Armands Circle. Yet, there is elegance and charm still left, and here and there a touch of "old Florida."

East of the Gulf Coast rush lies an area of another Florida endangered species, the Florida Cracker. The name derives from the sound of the bullwhips used by the English-Scottish cattle drivers who settled here in the mid-1800s. You can still drive the old Cracker Trail from Bradenton to Fort Pierce, but it will be on concrete and asphalt. An authentic Cracker village called "Cracker Country" is located on the Florida State Fairgrounds at I-4 and US 301 in Tampa, but is open only during the state fair.

Several ethnic groups add to the lure of Central West Florida. Ybor City in Tampa is still home to a large Cuban settlement, Greek sponge fishermen still work the waters off Tarpon Springs, and the Scots still blow their bagpipes at Dunedin.

All those cold fronts that blow across the Great Plains mellow out by the time they reach this part of Florida, as do the visitors. Wintertime can be bright blue skies and one-blanket nights, perfect golfing weather. Also, sunsets are so spectacular they rate special attention. At 5 p.m. everybody drops everything but their golf clubs and heads for an outdoor bar to toast the sunset. Pass-A-Grille down at the southern tip of St. Pete with its open air bistros rates tops for sunsets.

Although there are less than 200 miles between west coast and east coast, you can't miss the differences between the two. On Florida's west coast life does not revolve around Disney World, and old standby attractions that have been around forever are still very popular. Traffic can be a nightmare, but all in all, the people are more friendly and offer a heartfelt welcome.

## St. Petersburg–Homosassa Springs–Inverness– Brooksville–Tampa

*Alt. 19, St. Petersburg to Tarpon Springs, 28 miles*

*US 19, Tarpon Springs to Homosassa Springs, 40 miles*

*SH 490, Homosassa Springs to Inverness, 15 miles*

*US 41, Inverness to Brooksville, 29 miles*

*US 41, Brooksville to Tampa, 40 miles*

*Total miles, 152*

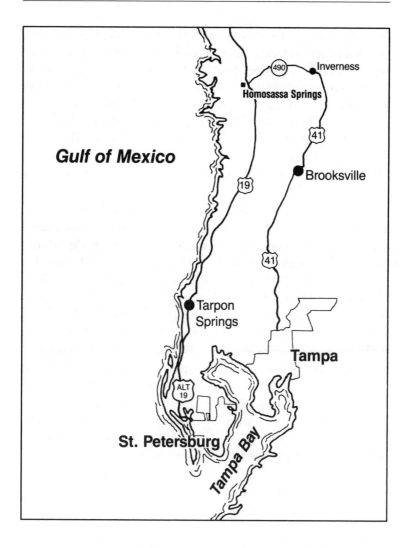

Like many Florida towns, St. Petersburg grew up around a railroad. When Peter Demens' Orange Belt Railroad crossed Florida, the Russian exile named this town at the end of the line for the city of his birth. For years, St. Pete had a reputation of catering to the old and ill, but all that has changed. While the spring break set doesn't whoop it up on St. Pete's Beach, the tourists are growing younger and younger. After you've seen St. Pete's famous inverted pyramid, The Pier, with its shops and restaurants, then go and say, "Hello, Dali," at the Salvador Dali Museum, 1000 Third Street South. You won't believe your eyes at the overwhelming collection of art by this eccentric genius. Neither will you believe the gift shop at Sunken Gardens, 1825 4th St. North. The gardens are lovely and boast more than 5,000 varieties of plants and hundreds of birds. The gift shop probably can't count the plethora of Florida souvenirs on display. It's huge and a fantastic example of "Florida tacky."

Look carefully for 18328 Gulf Boulevard in Indian Shores as you head north. Here is the Suncoast Seabird Sanctuary, Inc., and visitors are most welcome without charge. Wonderful volunteers are here to help with the rehabilitation of wild birds that have been injured. Most of these helpless birds were maimed by man's stupidity, and sadly, many will never return to the wild. You can't help but be impressed with the work done at the Sanctuary to rehabilitate the birds, and you will want to leave behind a generous donation.

Early Scottish immigrants founded Dunedin in 1870, and every March you can hear those bagpipes squealing during the Highland Games. Even if your ancestors didn't wear a kilt or have a clan tartan, you'll enjoy Dunedin Scottish Imports at 1401 Main Street. If it's Scottish you can probably find it here, except perhaps the dear little Scottish terrier dogs.

Across from Dunedin are two small getaway islands, Caladesi and Honeymoon. Caladesi can only be reached by ferry at the west end of State Road 586 and it is a little paradise of a spot with no cars. However, masked bandits are after your food, so raccoon-proof your baskets and coolers. Honeymoon Island got its name back in the '40s when developers built some palm-thatched huts and *Life* magazine sponsored free honeymoons. World War II saved the island from high rises, so you can now enjoy quiet beaches and watch ospreys build their nests: the kind of high rises you love to see under construction. Honeymoon Island is an easy jaunt via the Dunedin Causeway.

Shakespeare wrote, "It's all Greek to me," in his play *Julius Caesar,* but he could have had in mind Tarpon Springs. Tarpon Springs came into being in 1888, about the same time as St. Petersburg. The sponge beds in Key West were getting thin, so John Corcoris summoned his two brothers from Greece along with a lot of other Greeks who wanted to see the world. The title of Sponge Capital moved rapidly from Key West to Tarpon Springs.

You know it had to take guts, real guts, to go down in those old copper-helmeted diving suits, and many divers did end up using them as shrouds. Yet the industry grew, until after WWII and the invention of plastic sponges. Real sponges are for sale in the shops, and the Spongeorama Exhibit Center includes tours of the sponger's museum, factory, and village.

Strolling Tarpon Springs' streets and peering in the shops is a great way to spend a day. Restaurants serve marvelous seafood and Greek dishes, a bakery turns out fresh Greek bread, Saint Nicholas Greek Orthodox Cathedral is a replica of St. Sophia's in Constantinople, shops are filled with Greek exports, and you'll agree with the bard that "It's all Greek to me."

Aripeka, over on the Gulf on County Road 595, claims to be the last pioneer fishing village. A sign proclaims the town was named for the Seminole chief Aripeka, who was never defeated, and and also proclaims that village fishermen have always kept faith in the mercy and wrath of the sea. Ponce de Leon was here in 1513 and De Soto in 1539. But more recent tourists were Babe Ruth when he fished here in 1919, and Jack Dempsey when he was in training in 1921. Nowadays, it appears that famous visitors have dropped Aripeka from their itinerary.

Since 1947, live mermaids have been swimming in the clear cool waters of Florida's Weeki Wachee (904-596-2062). You can't miss the entrance; it is just past the 110-foot-long, 48-foot-high concrete dinosaur sitting by the side of the highway. One look, and you know that no paleontologist

*This dinosaur never made the textbooks, but he's part of the Florida landscape now.*

ever sculpted this big brontosaurus, or whatever this critter is from the prehistoric world.

Weeki Wachee, like many Florida names, is an Indian word. It means "winding waters" and refers to the river twisting and turning to the Gulf of Mexico. Owner Newton Perry was an ex-frogman, and he taught pretty young girls the art of breathing so they could remain below the surface without bobbing to the top and ruining their act. All they needed were mermaid outfits, and a show was born. You watch through 19-inch-thick plate glass windows, and new shows are presented regularly.

Another interesting show at Weeki Wachee is the Birds of Prey. Demonstrations by hawks, eagles, owls, vultures, and falcons give you a whole new perspective on these intelligent creatures. Just hope a grackle doesn't stroll by the falcon's cage when he is called on to perform because to a falcon, a grackle means "lunch," and makes a distracting temptation.

*Not all of the stars at Weeki Wachee Springs are mermaids. This little owl does his act at the "Birds of Prey" performance.*

## A WORD ON MANATEES

The big lovable manatee is in serious danger of extinction, and Florida is working hard to protect these rare mammals. There is absolutely nothing beautiful about a manatee, and how ancient seamen could think they were mermaids says a lot about being at sea too long.

About 60 million years ago, the manatee was closely related to the elephant, but somehow the manatee lost his trunk. Now, he has a short thick snout that literally would not hurt a flea, if manatees had fleas. These gentle animals grow 15 feet long and weigh more than 2,000 pounds, yet all they want to eat is some yummy lettuce, carrots, or water lilies.

During the winter, manatees need nice warm water and they will congregate in Florida's warm springs along the coast. With their sedentary habits and low reproductive rate, manatees are very vulnerable to man's carelessness and stupidity. More than 100 die each year due to encounters with motorboats or barges. A speeding motorboat can injure these big guys so badly they never recover. Even with a $500 fine for killing a manatee, boaters still will not be careful and watch for them. The public is invited to the Crystal River National Wildlife Refuge adjacent to the town of Crystal River. This refuge is especially for manatees and was acquired by the Nature Conservancy. The best time to view the manatees is from January to March.

Florida and conservation agencies sponsor a ''Manatee Adoption'' program, and for more information on these gentle giants, write Save The Manatee Club, 500 N. Maitland Ave., Maitland, FL 32751.

The Wilderness River Cruise at Weeki Wachee is nice and so is the Pelican Orphanage, and you'll love those plastic sculptures of King Neptune and family. A water park next door is sure-fire entertainment for the kids. Homosassa Springs Wildlife Park is quite unusual. Not only is this beautiful park a refuge for injured manatees, but you can go below the water's surface in the floating observatory to watch the manatees at close range. Whatever you do at Homosassa Springs, don't miss the manatee show. You will fall in love with these big huggable animals, as does everyone.

Amanda, Ariel, Hurricane, Rosie, Star, and Hugh absolutely crave attention from their handler. When she walks into the shallow water, here come the manatees. Manatees may not be as bright as dolphins or killer whales, but they know that box of manatee cookies their handler carries. With playful nudges, flapping of flippers, and lots of snorts, each manatee wants a cookie. The handler tells you the story of the manatees and why they are in the refuge as she rubs tummies, doles out cookies, and tries to keep her footing from the nudges of these gentle mammals. This show is absolutely delightful. Don't miss it!

These first magnitude springs flow 113.8 million gallons daily, and a zoo, nature trails, gardens, and river cruise complete the picture.

The Yulee Sugar Mill Ruins just down the road were once a part of a large plantation burned by Union troops during the Civil War.

A real crown jewel reigns over Inverness—The Crown Hotel, a 34-room, English-style inn that is a real Florida treasure (904-344-5555). In 1979, Reg Brealy, a British investor, spent $2.3 million to turn a rundown hotel into a proper English country inn. And, a proper inn it is. Replicas of the British crown jewels glitter in the lobby, high tea is served each day, bedrooms are like granny's house (provided you had a very rich granny), the Churchill Restaurant serves gourmet food, and the Fox and Hounds Pub is the perfect spot for the cocktail hour. Here is a romantic retreat you would expect to find on the heather of Scotland rather than the sawgrass of Florida.

One of the most pleasant things to do while visiting the Crown Hotel is to take a leisurely 10-mile canoe trip on the wide and winding Withlacoochee River (Little Great Water). It's almost as primitive and unspoiled as when DeSoto marked his trail through West Florida. Call Nobleton Canoe Outpost for rentals (904-796-4343).

If you really want to see the beauty of the Inverness area, drive north to Apopka to SH 470 and follow it around to SH 44 where you can head west back into Inverness.

On your way south toward Brooksville, take note of a 20-mile scenic Dogwood Trail through Chinsegut Hill National Wildlife Refuge and Withlacoochee State Forest. Plan to come back in the early spring for this outstanding drive.

Just off US 41 is the Dade Battlefield State Historic Site, where Major Francis L. Dade and his 100 men were massacred at the start of the Seminole Wars in 1835.

During the 1856 debate of the Kansas-Nebraska Bill, Massachusetts Senator Charles Sumner violently denounced Senator A. P. Butler of South Carolina. Butler was not present to defend himself, but his nephew Preston Brooks was. After adjournment, Brooks spotted Sumner in the Senate chamber, whipped out his newly polished gutta percha cane, and rapped it smartly over Sumner's head, leaving the senator unconscious on the floor. The southern states, Florida in particular, admired Brooks so much that the citizens of Hernando County voted to give the largest settlement his name.

Brooksville is a busy hub city where it is Christmas every day (except Christmas Day) at Rogers' Christmas House & Village, 103 Saxon Avenue (904-796-2415). Five houses glow with lights, trees, decorations, and gifts from all over the world. You can do all your Christmas shopping and decorating and never leave Rogers'. Can you believe a string of Holstein cow tree lights?

Masaryktown still celebrates Czechoslovakian Independence Day on the last Sunday of October with native foods and dancing. Czechs settled here in 1925 when the whole world knew who Jan Masaryk was.

It's not Disney World, but it's still mighty wonderful. Busch Gardens at the corner of Busch Boulevard and 40th Street (813-971-8282) is about eight miles northeast of downtown Tampa. Here is a trip to the Dark Continent with all of its mysterious jungles, sheiks of Morocco, exotic wildlife, and even a trip down the murky waters of the Congo.

*"Mueseli," a four-year-old female koala, samples her version of a buffet dinner in the koala display at Tampa's Busch Gardens where she regularly chooses her favorites from over 20 varieties of fresh eucalyptus.* © 1990 Busch Gardens, Tampa.

*A reticulated giraffe strikes her best pose for the camera while others enjoy a zoo attendant's's handouts on the 60-acre Serengeti Plain at Tampa's Busch Gardens.* © 1990 Busch Gardens, Tampa.

Busch Gardens is home to one of the largest collections of free-roaming wild animals in the United States. With more than 3,300 animals numbering some 340 species, Busch Gardens is a special place where learning about animals is fun. You can watch the Asian elephants get their daily bath (just stand way back), pet an 18-foot Burmese python, and watch the koalas chomp on their eucalyptus leaves. A tour of the 60-acre Serengeti Plain by monorail or by steam locomotive gives you a close-up view of Africa's antelopes, giraffes, elephants, and many other rare and endangered species.

Take a trip to the Kasbah of Morocco and watch the graceful skaters perform "Around the World on Ice" at the Marrakesh Theater. Visit Nairobi, the capital of Kenya, and enjoy the baby animals at feeding time. Timbuktu may

*Four geldings, a mare, and a foal are the featured residents in a new permanent display for Budweiser Clydesdales where visitors can enjoy a close-up view of these beautiful animals.* © 1990 Busch Gardens, Tampa.

sound like North Africa, but at Busch Gardens it's also German food and entertainment. And, of course, the famous Clydesdales are on parade. What would a Busch Brewery be without its magnificent horses!

Exotic food, carnival food, breath-gasping amusement rides, a water park, world-wide shopping, a bird show, a

*Fun seekers hang on tight as the Python roller coaster delivers its special brand of slithery high-speed excitement.* © 1990 Busch Gardens, Tampa.

dolphin show, and don't forget the brewery tour—all waiting for you at Busch Gardens.

The story of Florida is almost the story of railroad tycoons. In 1884, Henry B. Plant extended his South Florida Railroad to the mouth of the Hillsborough River and built the Tampa Bay Hotel. In an obvious effort to out-Flagler Flagler, Plant's Tampa Bay is a masterpiece of silver minarets topped by

Islamic crescents, and it dominates the city of Tampa. Plant hired rickshaws to carry guests around the opulent grounds, and even Flagler never thought of rickshaws. You are welcome to tour this bit of the Middle East through the restored section of the main floor which is the Henry Plant Museum, but most of the hotel is now a college.

About the time Plant arrived, so did Vincente Martinez Ybor. Ybor moved his cigar factory from Key West and men from Cuba came to roll those tobacco leaves into fine cigars. Ybor City became the center of the Hispanic community, and the streets pulsed with excitement as Cuban freedom fighter Jose Marti made thrilling speeches against Spain.

Teddy Roosevelt rode into Ybor City on his horse, Texas, with his dog, Cuba, and his Rough Riders. Meanwhile, the prostitutes on Last Chance Street entertained the soldiers waiting to embark to San Juan Hill.

Ybor City is definitely a lot quieter today. The prostitutes have disappeared, and the world of cigar smokers has almost disappeared as well. Ybor Square, one of the old cigar factories, is now a shopping mall and museum. Hundreds of workers used to sit at long benches, tediously rolling cigars. A "reader" sat on a platform above them and read to them from newspapers and books. To become a reader was a goal of many of the cigar rollers. Nearly 12,000 people once worked in more than 200 cigar factories. Cuban, Italian, Spanish, and German immigrants were seated on those benches, and all left their mark on Ybor City.

Automation killed the hand labor of Ybor City, but it is still a very historic little area with its turn-of-the-century street lamps and Spanish-style architecture. One enduring landmark that every visitor will enjoy is the Columbia Restaurant at 2117 7th Ave. (813-148-4961). Built in 1905 by Casimiro Hernandez, the Columbia now occupies an entire city block with eleven dining rooms and seating for up to 1,660 guests, plus Spanish dancers and guitarists.

The food is to die for. This gem of Spanish restaurants has received accolades from royalty, U. S. presidents, and most of

Hollywood. When you see the menu, you want it all. But, if time is limited, order the world-famous 1905 Salad and Paella a la Valenciana with Cuban Black Bean Soup. Oh, and there's the Cuban Sandwich, the Grilled Grouper Sandwich, Chilled Gazpacho, and . . . all served with that fabulous hot Cuban bread.

The Columbia also has restaurants in Sarasota, St. Augustine, Tampa, and St. Petersburg.

Another restaurant treat is Tampa's Bern's Steak House at 1208 S. Howard Ave. (813-251-2421). When you walk into this stark white box of a building, you have no idea what awaits you. The decor is not just red, it is very red. You are not sure if you're in a funeral parlor or a bawdy house. But, once your meal arrives, you could care less. Here is a steak in the grand manner.

Your quality steak is aged and you are given the vital statistics of each cut. Gert and Bern Laxer grow their vegetables on an organic farm, caviar is flown in regularly, and green coffee beans are hand sorted and then blended. But, enough about food. Bern's wine cellar is the envy of kings. About a half million bottles of wine line his racks. Just reading the wine list would take about a week, if you can lift it. For those who have always craved a Gruaud Larose 1833, it's yours for about $4,000 per magnum. If your tastes are more plebian, a glass of the house Chablis is a measly $4.50.

You can also come to Bern's just for dessert. The menu isn't as heavy as the wine list, but almost. You can get very cozy in one of 43 romantic dessert rooms made from old wine casks. If you want to watch the live entertainment while ''cast away,'' turn on the TV set in your cubbyhole to see who is tinkling the keys. Reservations are required for the restaurant and dessert rooms.

While on the subject of good food, just east of Tampa about ten miles on I-4 is the Branch Ranch. Numerous billboards give directions. The Branch family converted their modest bungalow into dining rooms in 1956, and it has grown like Topsy. This neat old house with its rather rustic decor has fed the multitudes such delicious downhome cooking they just keep coming back for more, and more and more. Order a main course of fried chicken, ham, prime rib, or lobster, and then get set for the avalanche: homemade sweet pickles, homemade marmalade, fresh veggies, and the world's best biscuits are just part of the entree. Try, try, try to save room for desserts, because they are homemade, too.

## TAMPA–SARASOTA–ARCADIA–ZOLFO SPRINGS

*US 41, Tampa to Sarasota, 39 miles*

*SH 72, Sarasota to Arcadia, 42 miles*

*US 17 Arcadia to Zolfo Springs, 23 miles*

*SH 64 (Cracker Trail), Zolfo Springs to I-75, 47 miles*

*Total miles, 151*

US 41, or the Tamiami Trail, might get a bit boring unless you like looking at shopping malls, so why not turn east on US 301 for 4 miles to the Gamble Plantation. Built in 1845, this is the oldest house on the West Florida Coast. Scarlett O'Hara would absolutely love it. Go back to US 41 and turn right on SH 64 at Bradenton. You'll come to the beautiful beaches of Anna Maria Island, where the Chamber of Commerce touts the shelling as better than Sanibel's. Check out the 1925 Harrington House (813-778-5444), a special bed and breakfast right on the beach. Head south on SH 789 and you'll find yourself on swanky St. Armands Circle. Restaurants and shops cater to Sarasota's affluent clientele.

Hernando de Soto was the first Spaniard to set foot on Sarasota soil, and according to legend, Sarasota was named after de Soto's daughter, Sara. This tidbit comes to you courtesy of the Sarasota Visitors Bureau.

For art lovers, Sarasota is the place. You'll wonder if you have arrived at a piazza in Venice or Florence, or perhaps walked into the Louvre in Paris. This superb museum was made possible by a bunch of clowns!

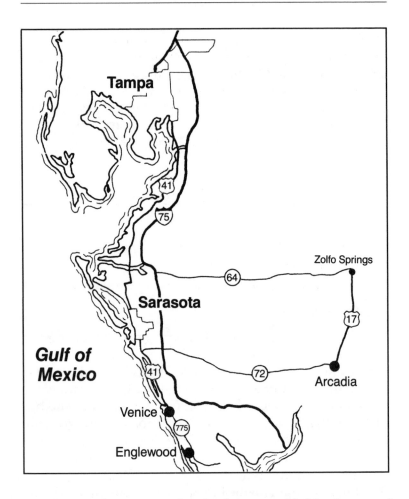

John Ringling accumulated a fortune with his circus and the "Greatest Show on Earth," and he didn't do badly with his investments in oil, real estate, and railroads. And, since an ostentatious display of wealth was in very good taste in the early '20s, John built a 30-room mansion patterned after the Doges' Palace in Venice, Italy. He named it *Ca'd'zan* which means "House of John" in Venetian, and gave it to his wife, Mabel, as a gift.

John and Mabel lived in absolute splendor, so much splendor they needed a museum to house it all. An edifice modeled on a fifteenth-century Florentine villa was deemed appropriate, and you can now view the most important collection of works by Peter Paul Rubens in the world. A bronze of Michaelangelo's David dominates exquisite formal gardens along with excellent copies of other masterpieces. John and Mabel certainly knew how to live.

Sarasota has another famous building, the nationally renowned Asolo State Theater. The interior was dismantled piece by piece from an opera house in Dunfermline, Scotland, then shipped to Sarasota in 1950. To see a performance in this ornate reconstructed opera house makes for a truly memorable evening.

A lovely little refuge tucked away on Sarasota's downtown waterfront on South Palm Avenue is the Selby Botanical Gardens. Take a self-guided tour of these beautiful gardens and you'll find that this is the first botanical garden in the world whose main emphasis is the study, research and display of epiphytic plants (in Latin, *epi* means upon, and *phyte* means plant). In other words, you will find just about every variety of air plant perched on trees and other plants. The Tropical Display House provides an introduction to the magnificence of tropical plants and a living classroom for studying them.

The rows and rows of malls south of Sarasota only seem endless. After about six miles, turn right onto Siesta Key and buy a T-shirt that brags, ''I have walked on the whitest finest sand in the world—Siesta Key.''

At Myakka River State Park, hop aboard the world's largest airboat and enjoy a scenic nature cruise on Myakka Lake. Because the *Gator Gal* is powered by air, you'll be able to explore shallow, grassy areas inhabited by alligators, great blue herons, sandhill cranes, anhingas, egrets, and many other species of waterfowl.

Another Myakka Wildlife Tour is offered aboard a special tram safari. Your land tour will take you off the park's main roads into remote subtropical forests and marshlands. No reservation is necessary for either tour.

If you get to Myakka early in the morning, you'll see one of the funniest sights in Florida. Perched all over the *Gator Gal*, the rental bicycles, parked cars with boat trailers, in the trees, and on fences is the most magnificent array of turkey buzzards you've yet to encounter. Try to count them. Just try it. They are everywhere and give the appearance that these are their boats, their bicycles, their cars, and their *Gator Gal*, and unless they get some handouts, they are not moving. All are very happy to pose for photographs, but the best picture may be the guy's face when he returns from fishing and sees his pickup truck where the buzzards have been roosting.

On the highway to Arcadia, contented cows graze peacefully under palm trees. Here is cowboy country, and Arcadia is basically a cow town with unusually wide streets

*Some of the happiest residents of Myakka State Park are the flocks of turkey buzzards that perch wherever they please.*

and arcaded sidewalks. You can count on rodeos in March and July. For some Florida peace and quiet, try a soothing canoe trip on the Peace River. From Arcadia you can chose a variety of different trips from Canoe Outpost, one mile northwest of Arcadia on SH 661 (813-494-1215). Weekends are *very* busy, and you might lose some of the river's peace and quiet.

Florida's promoters claim that the Sunshine State is fit for a king, but they probably did not have Howard Solomon in mind. Often called "the DaVinci of debris," Solomon worked more than twelve years to create his castle—complete with a 94-foot suspension bridge over the creek (no moat, however). You can hardly believe your eyes, but there it is. Iron gates, towers, turrets, stained glass windows (40 to be exact), earthworks, and of course, a dungeon. If you have a hard time accepting this "Debris Disney World" from the outside, just wait til you see what Solomon has accumulated inside—and he did it all in twelve years. Needless to point out, you'll absolutely love Howard Solomon, and he conducts his own tours. Bring your camera!

To visit this version of "one man's trash is another man's treasure," go west of Zolfo Springs on SH 64, then south on SH 665.

## SARASOTA–VENICE–ENGLEWOOD

*US 41 and SH 775, 28 miles*

If you haven't picked up on the problems with traffic on US 41, they do exist, but some sights are worth the trouble.

On Little Sarasota Bay in Osprey is a 30-acre environmental, archaeological and historic site featuring evidence of a sizable prehistoric Indian settlement with artifacts dating to 2150 B.C. Also, at Spanish Oaks there are pioneer homes and a museum. Mrs. Potter Palmer of the famous Chicago Palmer House Hotel invested a portion of her fortune in this area and built a fabulous winter residence. Long gone, only remnants of her retreat remain.

Everyone knows about Holiday Inns, but the Holiday Inn at 1660 S. Tamiami Trail in Osprey offers a lot of extra special features, including a really good restaurant and an excellent location for touring the area (800-HOLIDAY).

Big baskets, little baskets, silly baskets, expensive baskets, bargain baskets—they are all at 4011 Tamiami Trail (still on US 41) at Basketville. Other stuff is sold, too, but lots of Taiwanese have put in overtime on the baskets stacked on shelf after shelf after shelf.

Just about every town in Florida is "the capital" of something. Venice has its title, too. It's "the shark's tooth capital of the world." You can head for the beach and find your own, or stop by the Chamber of Commerce and get a package for free. The teeth would hardly inspire a new version of "Jaws," but how many places can you find real sharks' teeth? Caspersen Beach is wonderfully hidden away, so you might try searching its sands for those elusive teeth.

Venice, Florida, is a far cry from its sister city, Venice, Italy. The Florida version has no canals, no St. Mark's Square, no gondolas, and no Doges' Palace. But it does have a better climate. The whole town is very easygoing and comfortable. The big-money crowd has settled in Naples and Marco Island, so Venice still has its touch of charm.

Between Thanksgiving and early January, Ringling Brothers and Barnum & Bailey Circus comes home to Venice to rest. The performers create new routines, change their costuming, and give premiere showings to the local public. Clown College, founded in 1968, is the world's most outstanding institution for training professional clowns, and about 5,000 applicants vie for 60 spots in the classes each year.

Remember the movie *Sunset Boulevard*, with its opening scene of William Holden face down in the swimming pool—and dead? The mansion owned by Gloria Swanson was a '20s masterpiece, even if the owner was a bit daft. Reminiscent of the mansion in *Sunset Boulevard* is The Banyan

House Bed and Breakfast (813-484-1385), named for the enormous banyan tree in the yard. This historic home was built by one of the early founders of Venice, and the house even spent a few years as a paleontology museum. Today, The Banyan House is fit for Gloria and her Hollywood retinue, complete with swimming pool, but no dead body.

The big resort in Venice is The Plantation Golf & Country Club (800-826-4060). Golf, tennis, swimming, country club, fishing, and luxury homes put The Plantation right up there with Florida's top resorts.

Drive over to Casey Key with its quaint small motels and nice beach. The homes along the drive are on the affluent side, but Casey Key is still rather like an undeveloped Captiva Island.

For the budget-minded, 12 miles south of Venice on US 41 is Warm Mineral Springs (813-426-1692). Talk about "Old Florida," here it is at Warm Mineral Springs, in more ways than one. Underneath these 87-degree waters archaeologists have recovered the 10,000-year-old bones of a sabre-toothed cat and Paleo-Indian remains that are counted among the very oldest in North America. As you soak away your aches and pains in Florida's only warm springs, you can watch the divers at work recovering more artifacts. Sonny Cockrell is in charge of the "dive-dig," and you will find his stories fascinating.

Folks come out with lawn chairs, take a little dip in the mineral-rich springs and spend the day gossiping. The massage facilities and snack bar are on the premises, but the one-bedroom apartments are back on the highway. The buildings look like '40s or early 50's vintage, but the actual springs are on the National Register of Historic Places.

Manasota Key is a designated wildlife preserve, yet is accessible by two bridges to the towns of Venice and Englewood. Only seven miles long, its winding, tree-covered road goes through quiet, residential areas. Try one of the Manasota Beach Club's fifteen cottages, some which have been on the beach since the early 1900s (813-475-6711). Year after year, Manasota Key has been left off the Florida

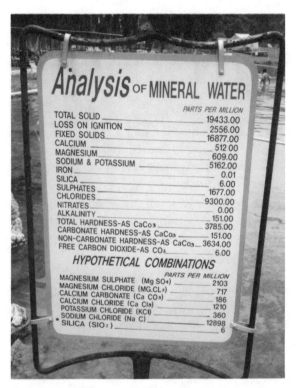

*Florida's crystal-clear springs are world-renowned. Join the folks that frequent these bubbling waters and become a "spring hopper," too.*

maps, and during the summer months the sign is taken down so you can't find it. The owners go back north and shut down completely until the main season from October until the end of May. You can call them in Rhode Island at 401-322-0301; ask for Robert Buffum.

# REGION 4

# CENTRAL
# FLORIDA

If you believe that kingdoms and royalty are limited to other continents, then you have never been to Central Florida. In 1967, the Florida legislature created a world unlike any place on earth. It granted a private corporation the privilege to turn 42 square miles of land, twice the area of Manhattan, into a kingdom, complete with corresponding powers. Its official name was Walt Disney World Vacation Kingdom, but now it is famous as Disney World.

When King Mickey and his entourage arrived in Orlando in October of 1971, the face of Florida changed forever. Old, tried-and-true Florida attractions were forgotten in the glitter and glory of the Magic Kingdom, EPCOT, MGM Studios, and all the other tourist delights that coast along on Mickey's magic. It is absolutely mind-boggling to imagine what it would cost a family of four to stay in Orlando long enough to partake of every attraction offered, not including the plethora of gift shops.

Old Floridians love and hate King Mickey. In spite of the benefits and problems Disney World created, they all know that if it weren't for that delightful mouse, not much would be left of Florida tourism today.

But, there was a wonderful world of Florida long before Mickey. With its numerous lakes and springs, Central Florida still draws almost as many tourists as its beaches. Up around Ocala, the gentle rolling hills are home to many thoroughbred horses. Instead of the white beaches, you see miles of white fences around verdant pastures. Historic towns like Mt. Dora, Lake Wales, and Sanford manage to retain their old-time aura in spite of increased population and the proximity of Disney World.

So, when you've worn out your shoes and your nerves from the high tech of Orlando, slip away to an easier pace

*Watch out, Kentucky! Florida's thoroughbred Industry is booming.* Photo © Mark J. Barrett.

at Silver Springs or Cypress Gardens or the melodious Bok Tower. Head for the backroads when you do and experience Florida in the days before King Mickey ruled the realm. The charm is still there, just a little more difficult to find.

## ORLANDO

Much has been written on Orlando and Disney World because the area is growing and changing constantly. Yet, Orlando is an ideal location for your Florida vacation headquarters. For those who are ready to spend big bucks on a hotel but want something away from the Disney World conglomorate, try the Peabody. (800-PEABODY). Made famous by its antique ancestor in Memphis, Tennessee, the Orlando Peabody has carried on its Memphis tradition by having live ducks preen and swim in the lobby fountain. Everyday at 10 am and 4 pm, these delightful ducks parade down a red carpet: to the fountain in the morning, and in the evening, to the elevator where they are whisked away

*Their names aren't Donald, Dippy, or Dewey, but these ducks are famous, too. They are the residents of the fountain in the lobby of Orlando's Peabody Hotel.*

to the "duck hotel" on the roof. Rooms and restaurants are absolutely first class at the gorgeous Peabody Hotel.

It is a rare American household kitchen that doesn't have at least one piece of Tupperware, and how many housewives in the '50s and '60s could say they had never been to a Tupperware party? Well, off the beaten path to Disney World is the Tupperware International Headquarters on US 441 in Orlando. Visitors are guided on a personal tour including the colorful model kitchen demonstrating the convenience and versatility of Tupperware brand products. Also, a real treat at the end of the Tupperware showcases is a museum of containers used by man dating from an Egyptian pot from 4000 B.C. to the present. Exhibits encompass Chinese dynasties, American Indians, English china, and American pewter—just to name a few. And, at the end of your tour you are given a Tupperware memento to add to the rest of your kitchen collection. For tour information, call (407-847-3111). It's fun, it's educational, and it's free.

Another Orlando attraction just next door to Tupperware at 14501 South Orange Blossom Trail (US 441) is Gatorland Zoo. You can't miss it. You enter through the mouth of a

*For this Florida version of* Jaws, *don't miss Gatorland.*

gigantic alligator, complete with all of its teeth. As you travel around Florida you'll find quite a number of alligator farms and unless you really love these big grinning reptiles, just visit Gatorland. You'll see 5,000 of the critters all the way from just hatched to their ultimate fate as boots, belts and wallets. And, 5,000 is a lot of alligators. Remember the alligator frenzy in the movie *Indiana Jones and the Temple of Doom?* It was filmed here.

Gatorland was founded in 1949 with a few huts and a handful of alligators. Now, Gatorland has grown to 35 acres, and it has a scenic 2,000-foot walkway through the Cypress Swamp where you can see animals in their natural environment. The big feature is the "Gator Jumparoo." As dead chickens are strung out over the gator pool, suddenly with a flash of deadly teeth, a monstrous alligator will leap high

*Gatorland's stars are big, green, ugly, and mean.*

out of the water and snatch the meat off the line. Gulp! It's gone! You have to be fast to catch this mouthful on film.

If you want to see a man eating alligator, come to the Great Gator Cookoff in April. You can pick up some prizewinning recipes for gator meat from some of the outstanding chefs of the area. These culinary experts will be doing their utmost to make gator meat tasty, because the grand prize is a trip to Europe. The Gatorland Gift Shop also sells Gator Chowder and Gator Sauce.

## ORLANDO–WINTER PARK–SANFORD–WEKIWA SPRINGS

*I-4, Orlando to Winter Park (Orange Ave. Exit, SH 426), 10 miles*

*SH 426 to SH 436 to US 17, Winter Park to Sanford, 20 miles*

*I-4, Sanford to Orlando, 30 miles*

*Total miles, 60*

For a while during the early 1980s, Winter Park was known as "Sinkhole City." A sinkhole suddenly opened up in the middle of town and proceeded to swallow an auto repair shop, six cars, part of two streets, the deep end of the local swimming pool, and the home and yard of one of the town's residents. When it finally finished devouring a section of Winter Park, the hole was 350 feet across and 100 feet deep.

The affluent residents of Winter Park never liked the nickname, so no reference is made to "Sinkhole City" in any of the town's brochures. Winter Park prefers being known for its prestigious Rollins College, fine homes, and very select shops on Park Avenue. Park Avenue boasts finer shops with more snob appeal than even Palm Beach.

Nestled among the elegant shops is the Charles Hosmer Morse Museum of American Art. There is art glass in this world, and then there is Tiffany art glass. Get ready to feast your eyes on the largest collection of Tiffany glass and jewelry

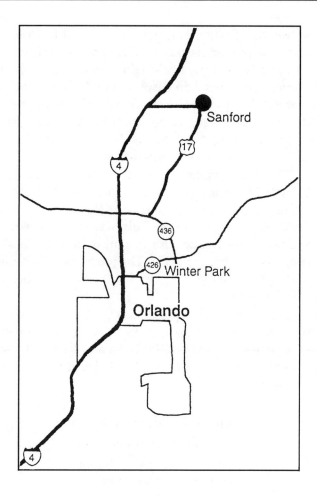

in the world. Who wants to shop when you can admire this breathtakingly beautiful display of Tiffany's finest art?

Rollins College is among the top ten of America's small colleges, and though you may not think of a college campus tour as part of your Florida experience, the Walk of Fame is well worth your time. The Walk is bordered by 800 stones brought from the homes and birthplaces of famous people. You may not recognize all 800 inscriptions, but you will know most of them.

Also on the Rollins campus is the Beal-Maltbie Shell Museum. The seas are home to more than two million types of shells, and here at the Beal-Maltbie you can see them all, plus numerous oddities on display. The Chinese once used shells for window glass. The Hindus considered some shells sacred. And, shell sizes range from fingernail-tiny to the 300-pound drinking fountain at the entrance. For shell lovers, this museum is an absolute must.

In 1937, Orson Wells scared the daylights out of the country with his broadcast, "War of the Worlds." Kate Smith sang "God Bless America," and Bugs Bunny said, "What's up, Doc?" for the first time. This was also the year that Scenic Boat Tours opened for business in the "Venice of America," Winter Park, Florida. The tours are still operating, and you learn all that 1937 trivia from their present brochure. Call (407-644-4056).

It is fun to cruise the quiet lakes and canals lined with mansions old and not so old. Gardens bloom profusely along the banks and ancient live oaks and cypress trees add to the beauty of the lakes. As Roy I. Hoppman (whoever he was) said,

On Morse Boulevard at lakeside
By a pathway leading down,
Just a little bit of walking
From the center of town,
Ship, Ahoy! A boat awaits you,
Are you ready to embark
For a pleasant trip by water
Touring scenic Winter Park?

A posh little inn right on Park Avenue is the Park Plaza Hotel (407-647-1072). No two rooms are alike, and the decor is antiques, wicker, and a plethora of potted plants. The inn's delightful restaurant is the Park Plaza Gardens, famous for its Sunday Brunch.

For another cruise of a different magnitude, how about steamboatin' on the St. Johns River on the *Grand Romance*? Talk about a memorable Florida experience, here's one you don't want to miss (800-225-7999). You embark from Sanford on Lake Monroe and head up the St. Johns for your river adventure. You can take your choice of two-day cruises or three-hour cruises. Or, perhaps you are one of those romantic souls who prefer the moonlight on a dinner cruise. Regardless, *Grand Romance* will entertain you royally with a floor show, dancing, cash bar, and tons of superb food. It's a bit hard to watch the scenery outside for the music and fun inside.

A good idea is to arrive in Sanford a day early and visit the Central Florida Zoo. It's not big, but it is clean, and kids love it. For a bit of Florida history, take the Sanford walking tour. The town goes back to 1870 when General Henry S. Sanford decided to develop the citrus industry. Citrus never made the big time, but celery did, and today Sanford is the Celery Capital of the World. Just south of Sanford on US 17-92 is Flea World, with more than 1,000 dealers and open on weekends. A nice place to stay in Sanford is just across from the *Grand Romance* at the Holiday Inn. You're right in the heart of historic Sanford.

On your return to Orlando, stop by Big Tree Park. Located in Longwood on General Hutchinson Parkway, one mile west of US 17-92 is the world's oldest and largest cypress tree, a specimen more than 3,500 years old. At the base, the circumference is 54 feet, and it stands 127 feet tall. It was 165 feet tall, but a hurricane in 1926 lopped off a few feet.

Just west of Longwood is Wekiwa Springs, and this is a very special park because somehow it has managed to survive the encroachment of subdivision after subdivision. Florida has protected the Wekiva River by designating it as an Outstanding Florida Waterway and part of the river as Scenic and Wild. It flows through 20,000 acres of state-owned lands and as you paddle beneath its dense green canopy, city life seems thousands of miles away. It is hard to believe that the interstate is just "over there."

The Timucan Indians may have lived along the river for as long as 7,500 years, and their middens dot the shores of the Wekiva. (You will see Wekiwa spelled also as Wekiva. The name comes from the Creek-Seminole word meaning "the waters of the springs." Now the maps designate the springs as Wekiwa and the river as Wekiva, but it is still a subject for debate.)

The flora and fauna along the Wekiva River are gorgeous, and you realize this is how Florida must have looked long before the Spanish arrived. Rare plants and endangered animals are not easy to spot, but they still survive in this pristine environment. Even Florida black bears still roam the woods along the river.

Just up the river from the park is the Wekiwa Marina with canoe rentals, a cruise boat, and a restaurant specializing in catfish dinners.

## ORLANDO–MT. DORA–OCALA (Silver Springs)

*US 441, Orlando to Mt. Dora, 26 miles*

*US 441, Mt. Dora to Ocala, 41 miles*

*SH 40, Ocala to Silver Springs, 1 mile*

*I-75 and Turnpike, Ocala to Orlando, 55 miles*

*Total miles, 125*

On your way up busy US 441, slow down as you get to Plymouth, three miles north of Apopka. Look for the big billboard inviting you to visit Florida Cactus, Inc. and take them up on the invitation. Exit US 441 west on Boy Scout Blvd. and follow the signs. The greenhouses are on S. Peterson Road. Feel free to browse in all of the potting rooms on your own and then take your purchases to the office for payment.

When you think of Florida, you think of palm trees, orange groves, and other tropical flora. You certainly don't expect deserts and cactus. Surprise! Here at Florida Cactus you will find just about every variety you can imagine.

Greeting you is a 24-by-12-foot map of the United States made of cacti with a different variety representing each state. Also, you can't miss the electric clock (75-foot circumference) made of 10,000 yellow, pink, red, green, and orange cacti. It

even keeps perfect time. You certainly won't find these arrangements in your average cactus garden.

Mt. Dora has the distinction of being one of the Sunshine State's highest elevations—184 feet above sea level. The town's first name was Royellou, a combination of the first names of the three children of an early pioneer family; but it was changed to Mt. Dora in 1883. A definite New England flair prevails in this quaint little city, and historic buildings are everywhere. You know you have found a special place when a town calls itself "The Antique Center of Central Florida."

Just beyond downtown is Lake Dora where a continual procession of graceful sailboats skims the waves. And, on the banks of this small lake is the fabulous Lakeside Inn (800-556-5016). Established in 1883, during the '20s and '30s the inn served as the winter home for such personages as President and Mrs. Calvin Coolidge. Now restored to its

*You won't find any deserts in Florida, but for real beauty, enjoy Plymouth's cactus garden.*

original English Tudor splendor, the inn offers 87 beautifully appointed rooms with no two alike.

Mt. Dora is an ideal place to experience an escape to yesterday.

It was around 7 am, January 16, 1935 when Oklawaha, Florida, exploded into national notoriety. Oklawaha had always thought of the Blackburns as quiet, well-mannered tourists. Yet, on this quiet January day, an estimated 3,000 rounds of rifle, shotgun, and machine-gun fire shattered the white, two-story lakefront home the Blackburns rented. For four hours the battle raged between the F. B. I. agents and the occupants of the house. When the chaos was over, the riddled bodies of the notorious Ma Barker and her son Fred lay dead on the second floor. Ma and her gang were into kidnapping, killing, and stealing and hiding out as tourists in Florida. Oklawaha, Florida, made headlines across the nation for the first and last time in its history.

If you would like to see the site of this incredible carnage, take SH 42 east from US 441 around Lake Weir to Oklawaha. Turn west toward the lake after passing the Oklawaha Methodist Church. The house is at the end of the drive right on the lake, or just ask anyone in Oklawaha about Ma and Fred. The bullet holes have been patched.

Marion County is ranked as the third-fastest-growing county in the nation, and you can easily understand why folks want to move here. Scenic rolling hills, oak and pine hammocks, and spring-fed lakes all add to the beauty of this popular Florida area. Named for Francis Marion, the famous "Swamp Fox" of Revolutionary War fame, the county's first industry was citrus groves. Because of the hard freezes, the county is now famous for its 490 beautiful horse farms and racetrack winners. To visit some of these breeding farms, contact the Florida Thoroughbred Breeders' Association for a brochure (904-629-2160).

Ocala's Chamber of Commerce (904-629-8051) will be glad to send you information on the area. You can watch a smashing game of jai-alai (a game invented by Basque peasants and played with a woven glove that looks like a six-foot toucan's beak), visit the only museum of drag racing in the world, and swim at Juniper, Alexander, and Salt Springs. One spring you have to visit is the famous old Silver Springs. Now a Registered National Landmark, Silver Springs was Florida's first tourist attraction (800-342-0297).

During the Civil War, Silver Springs was a significant shipping point for Confederate Army goods, but following the war, the Oklawaha and Silver Rivers began to carry a richer cargo—tourists. And, the tourists have never stopped coming to view "nature's wonderland." Mary Todd Lincoln, Harriet Beecher Stowe, and William Cullen Bryant loved Silver Springs and were duly impressed with these first magnitude springs that flow 532 millions gallons daily.

Silver Springs really hit the big time back in the '30s and '40s when Johnny Weismuller and Maureen O'Sullivan arrived to film six of the Tarzan movies. Johnny whooped and hollered and swung on vines (actually ropes) all over Silver Springs. Maureen looked fetching in her very short animal-skin dress and her hair never ruffled. Every tourist in Florida back then put Silver Springs tops on his list to visit.

Movies are still filmed here at the Springs, but lots of changes have taken place since Johnny and Maureen and Cheetah climbed those trees. The historic glass-bottomed boats continue to glide the crystal-clear waters and the animal shows still delight audiences of all ages, but now you can take a Jungle Cruise on quiet electric boats to view exotic wildlife from six continents. After the cruise, experience the newest attraction, the Jeep Safari. Visitors love this ride among free-roaming wildlife in natural habitats. Just watch for the resident troop of rhesus monkeys, the only wild troop in North America. According to the story, a few of these critters got loose during one of Johnny and Maureen's movies and settled down to stay.

Silver Springs offers much more—an antique car museum, a water park, restaurants, and gift shops. You will want to return again and again.

Ocala's Historic District contains 207 buildings, and the entire district is on the National Register of Historic Places. If you have booked a room at the Seven Sisters Inn, circa 1888, (904-867-1170), you will stay at one of Florida's finest B&Bs. How long has it been since you slept on ironed antique cotton sheets? And, when did you last dine on baked eggs with caviar for breakfast? The inn was originally owned by Norma Johnson who named each room for one of her seven sisters. The present owners are Ken Oden and Bonnie Moorehardt, and elegance still prevails.

*Silver Springs' glass-bottomed boats were entertaining visitors even before Johnny Weismuller arrived to film his Tarzan movies.*

A slight detour well worth the time on your return to Orlando is Clermont. Right off US 27 is the Lakeridge Winery & Vineyards. The Spanish-style winery opened in 1989 and uses all Florida-grown grapes with the expectation of producing some 150,000 gallons of wine a year. Take the tour and then sample the Lakeridge wines in the handsome tasting room and gift shop.

Also at Clermont is the old Florida Citrus Tower. Built in 1956, it looks rather tacky and seedy now, but if you take the

*Silver Springs' beauty isn't all under water. Now you can tour the exotic animal park in jeeps.*

elevator up the 226-foot tower, you will see about 2,000 square miles of orange trees. Unfortunately, not all of them will be alive, because the freezes have been brutal to the citrus industry.

The orange came to the New World with Columbus on his second voyage in 1493. He planted the Seville orange in Haiti, and from there it was carried throughout the Caribbean by the Spanish explorers. Historians believe the orange arrived around 1579 in St. Augustine. The Timucan Indians loved the fruit and deliberately scattered the seeds throughout northern Florida. Citrus culture began in the northern part of Florida simply because the southern part of the state was sparsely populated. Micanopy, McIntosh, Mandarin, and Windsor were prosperous citrus communities prior to the Great Freeze of 1894–95.

The freezes did not stop in 1894–85, and each year more and more citrus groves are destroyed either by weather or canker infestation. Unlike other fruits, the orange has to ripen for about 300 days "on the vine" and in the sun. It cannot be picked early and allowed to mature in a bin. So, a freeze of even the slightest duration is usually devastating.

Along this area the highway is lined with fruit stands selling everything from orange candy to orange wine, plus T-shirts.

## ORLANDO–LAKELAND–LAKE WALES

*I-4, Orlando to Lakeland, 32 miles*

*US 98, Lakeland to Bartow, 12 miles*

*SH 60, Bartow to Lake Wales, 15 miles*

*Alt. US 27, Lake Wales to Babson Park, 8 miles*

*US 27, Lake Wales to I-4, 26 miles*

*I-4 to Orlando, 18 miles*

*Total miles, 111*

ALTERNATE

*US 27, Lake Wales to Sebring, 32 miles*

ALTERNATE

*SH 60 east, Lake Wales to Outdoor Resorts River Ranch, 25 miles*

One of the most controversial men in America during the 1930s was the renowned architect Frank Lloyd Wright. He had an admirer in Dr. Ludd M. Spivey, president of Florida Southern College in Lakeland from 1925 to 1957. In 1936, Dr. Spivey conceived the idea of an ultramodern campus designed by Wright. Ground was broken two years later for the first of twelve buildings (the Annie Pfeiffer Chapel) for Florida Southern, the largest collection of Frank Lloyd Wright designs in the world. Signs throughout Lakeland direct you to the campus, and a walking tour of the campus is available at the Emile E. Watson Administration Building. You don't need a brochure to tell you which twelve buildings were designed by Wright. Each is so distinctive and so unique even a novice can pick them out.

Down around Bartow you will find that the landscape suddenly looks like a moonscape. This barren wasteland is Bone Valley, home of Florida's phosphate mines. About ten million years ago the ocean flooded this area. Billions of phosphate particles (formed possibly from sea life excreta, from the remains of tiny sea organisms, or of inorganic

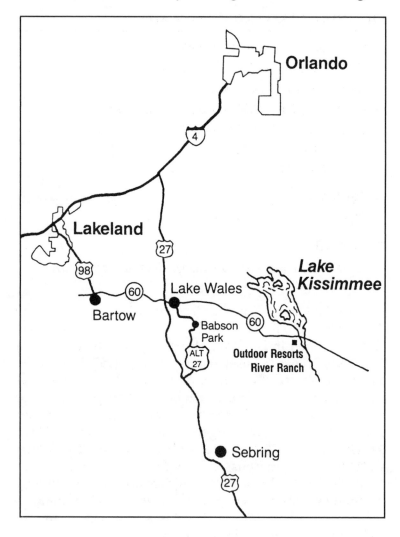

origins) were deposited on this ocean floor. These particles along with sand and clay settled into strata. It is now known as Bone Valley because of the bones and fossilized remains of prehistoric animals found in the deposits. The Mulberry Phosphate Museum in downtown Mulberry has an outstanding collection of the fossils found in the area. Needless to say, Bone Valley is a subject of intense controversy among Florida's ecologists.

Lake Wales, at 250 feet above sea level, is one of the highest folds of earth in Florida. It is also one of the most terrific little towns in the Sunshine State. Rising another 205 feet and overlooking the town is Bok Tower on Alt. US 27 east of town. This marble and coquina tower atop Iron Mountain looks like a structure that should be next to a European cathedral, yet close inspection reveals the sculptures are of Florida wildlife.

Edward Bok, an early editor of "Ladies Home Journal," donated this tower to Florida in 1929. This Dutch immigrant "wanted to make America more beautiful because he had lived in it," and he is buried at the foot of his beloved tower.

Visiting the Bok Tower and its 128-acre garden is an almost religious experience. Here is one of the world's great carillons with 57 bronze bells ranging in weight from 17 pounds to 12 tons. Carillonneur Milford Myhre performs a daily recital at 3 pm. The gardens are designed for thought and reflection and a quiet escape from a raucous world.

Lake Wales is also the winter home of the Black Hills Passion Play, which reconstructs the dramatic events of the last seven days of the life of Christ. The play runs from February to mid-April. You may write for tickets (Passion Play, Box 71, Lake Wales, FL 33859) or call 813-676-1495.

A different sort of attraction is Lake Wales' eerie Spook Hill. Just off of Alt. US 27 (watch for signs) and North Avenue is the weird phenomenon of Spook Hill. Park your car on the white line at the bottom of the hill, release the brakes and clutch and watch your car roll uphill by itself. No explanation is available unless you like an Indian legend that sounds like it was made up by the local Chamber of Commerce.

Many moons ago, Seminole chief Cufcowellax and his people lived happily on Lake Wales, but then a huge bull alligator slithered in and began to make nightly raids. The tribe lived in terror of this evil spirit. For many suns Cufcowellax tried to trap the monstrous 'gator until finally the chief caught his foe asleep. They engaged in a battle that lasted for a moon, and the water of the lake turned red, but Cufcowellax won. And, the reason cars now roll uphill is that the 'gator is seeking his revenge, or the chief is still protecting his land from the white man. Anyway, no logical explanation exists for Spook Hill.

One of the most charming places to stay and to dine in the entire state is at Chalet Suzanne on the outskirts of Lake Wales (813-676-6011). Back in 1931 when the whole world seemed to be poor, Bertha Hinshaw turned her home into an inn and dining room to support her two children. World

*If you don't believe the legends, think of another explanation as your car coasts uphill.*

War II saw another disaster for the Chalet when the main building, including the kitchen and many dining rooms, burned. But Bertha put together the horse stable, rabbit hutches, and frames of chicken houses and Chalet Suzanne was reborn—on 14 different levels. Today, you have an enchanting inn of 30 rooms on a 70-acre estate with its own landing strip and swimming pool, plus some of the finest gourmet food in the Southeast.

Just as no two rooms are alike in the inn, no two tables are set alike in the dining rooms. Dinner by candlelight on china from the family collection of English or German porcelain or perhaps Italian pottery or elegant Limoges creates a gorgeous atmosphere that cannot be duplicated. Guidebooks rate the Chalet with four stars for its baked grapefruit, hot potato rolls, crepes suzette, fabulous entrees, and luscious desserts—all accompanied by classic selections of wine. Film star Vincent Price found the Chalet's menu and setting absolutely superb. His signature is etched on one of the ceramic tiles made at the Chalet for the "Wall of Fame" in the garden.

The Chalet's soups are so good that a cannery has been built on the premises, and you may purchase cans of those savory soups. Astronaut Jim Irwin and the crew of Apollo 15 took Chalet Suzanne soups on their flight to the moon.

Bertha's son Carl Hinshaw and his wife Vita now run the Chalet just as Bertha would want, with wonderful food and wonderful Florida hospitality. Make Chalet Suzanne your headquarters for touring Central Florida.

Just 10 minutes away from Lake Wales in Winter Haven is the old Florida attraction that began drawing tourists back in the 1930s. The Dick Pope family cultivated moss-draped cypress, fields of flowers, pools, and grottoes and called it Cypress Gardens. In 1942, the world famous "Greatest American Water Ski Show" was added making it a top Florida attraction. Cypress Gardens continues to enchant visitors with its beauty. Anheuser-Busch now owns this theme park, and many new attractions enhance Cypress Gardens.

If time is limited at Cypress Gardens, put the "Greatest American Water Ski Show" at the top of your list. The talent displayed by these marvelous skiers is just incredible. Also amazing you with their skill and precision are the performers in the "Classical Ice Show" and the "Air Dancing" acrobatic extravaganza.

*You will agree with Vincent Price that Chalet Suzanne is one of Florida's premier historic inns.*

In the early 1940s a killer freeze swept through Central Florida and damaged the plants at the entrance of Cypress Gardens. Visitors began leaving before even buying a ticket thinking that all of the gardens had suffered as a result of the freeze. Julie Pope ingeniously dressed some of the pretty employees in Southern Belle costumes and placed them at the park entrance. Since that day, the tradition of southern hospitality is still embodied by these lovely girls, and they are among the most-photographed women in the world.

Wear your heavy-duty walking shoes for your visit to Cypress Gardens. You have to browse the gift shops, take pictures at the Animal Forest, go up in the Kodak Island in the Sky for a breathtaking view of the gardens, and stroll 223 acres of natural beauty with 8,000 varieties of plants and flowers.

If you have thoughts of matrimony, what more spectacular setting for a wedding? It can be arranged at Cypress Gardens. On your way down to Sebring, take Alt. US 27 through Frostproof (don't you love the name?!) You'll wind around some lakes and go through Babson Park. Chalet Suzanne may be a bit rich for your pocketbook, but check out Hillcrest Lodge (813-638-1712). The rates are considerably lower, the food is absolutely delicious, and the lodge is right on Lake Caloosa. Owners Martha and R. H. Wetzel spend their summers on Lake Erie up in Yankeeland, but they return every October for guests who visit year after year.

Sebring ranks with Indianapolis, Daytona, and Le Mans in the world of auto racing. Thousands of spectators are drawn to the 12-Hour Endurance Race held each March on the grueling 4.11 mile Airport Race Course. Sporty Porsches and Maseratis spin a dizzying course around this track loaded with hairpin turns.

For a folksy habitat that makes you part of the family, try the Santa Rosa Inn in downtown Sebring (813-385-0641). Built in 1924, all of the guest rooms are different in style and you will feel welcome and comfortable.

Located 6 miles west of Sebring on SH 634 is one of Florida's four original state parks, Highland Hammock (813-385-0011). Alligators and exotic flora can be seen from a "trackless train" that tours the swamps and jungles of this popular park. Hiking trails wander through its 3,800 acres, and a special paved trail is just for bikers. Keep your eyes peeled—you may see a Florida panther. These highly endangered cats have actually been spotted here, but not very often.

Just 25 miles east of Lake Wales is the nation's first and only guest ranch and RV resort: Outdoor Resorts River Ranch (Florida, 800-282-7935, nationwide, 800-282-7935). Actually, you don't have to have an RV to enjoy this dude ranch. Your plane is welcome on the 5,000-ft lighted airstrip. Then, you can book a room in the River Ranch Inn, or a one- or two-bedroom cottage with fireplace. RVers are offered manicured, full-service sites shaded by live oaks and palm trees.

So, get out of your RV or car and have the friendly wrangler saddle up Silver and trot off with a "Hi ho and away" for a leisurely horseback ride. Then, you can amble over to the health club and the bones that didn't fit Silver's gait will probably fit better in the hot tub.

River Ranch has it all—pool, fishing, hunting, dancing, restaurant, bar, game room, and outdoor activities. All you need are your comfortable duds and a love of the great outdoors.

# CENTRAL EAST FLORIDA

The fastest cars in the world zoom around the Daytona International Speedway. A space shuttle thrills the world as the count comes down to liftoff at Cape Canaveral. No matter where you go on Florida's central east coast, it's a blast!

It's just almost impossible to find some backroads in this crowded area of Florida. Daytona boasts "The World's Most Famous Beach"—at least according to the throngs of spring break-ers who have traditionally flocked to this youthful resort city to create their own version of a wild life refuge.

Stretching some 23 miles along the Atlantic from Ormond Beach to New Smyrna Beach, the beach at various points is up to 500 feet wide but still filled with sun lovers. New Smyrna Beach is considered the "World's Safest Beach" because rock ridges offshore prevent dangerous ocean undercurrents. New Smyrna Beach is much more laid back than Daytona Beach, and the 1886 Riverview Hotel (904-428-5858) on the Indian River has been beautifully restored with an excellent restaurant.

It was near Ponce Inlet that the automobile engine was developed after the turn of the century. During the '30s and '40s, the whole world waited every time an automobile raced along the beach trying for a new speed record. It follows that the Daytona International Speedway is among the world's best-known racetracks. When a race is underway, you can hear the engines whining and screaming all over town.

Ormond Beach also had its share of speedsters. Those wide sand beaches were a lot flatter and faster than the roads when the automobile was being perfected. Men named Chevrolet or Olds, Ford, Oldfield, or Winton were coming down and setting records for fast driving while the Rockefellers and Vanderbilts were content to watch from their mansions. In fact, John D. Rockefeller spent more than 20 winters at his home, known as The Casements, in Ormond Beach.

At NASA Kennedy Space Center's Spaceport U.S.A., there is no fee for admission, parking, or the extensive facilities. You will come away ready to sign up for the next shuttle to Mars.

All along this eastern seaboard of Florida are posh resorts, condos and bumper-to-bumper traffic. You will probably find I-95 a welcome relief from the congestion of US 1 and SH A1A. A few state parks offer oases, but even they are very popular.

Down around Fort Pierce, in centuries past, the treacherous ocean caused countless Spanish galleons to be wrecked. Now this area is nicknamed the Treasure Coast. Naturally, treasure-seeking divers love this part of the Atlantic and the UDT-SEAL Museum at 3300 North Route A1A in Fort Pierce. The museum honors the Underwater Demolition Teams and Sea, Air, and Land teams of the U. S. Navy.

In the very affluent town of Vero Beach, you can check in at a most unusual motel called the Driftwood Inn (407-231-0550). Literally, part of the inn is actually built of driftwood. During the 1930s, a legendary Florida eccentric, Waldo Sexton, constructed the Driftwood Inn and the Ocean Grill and

*The Driftwood Inn is appropriately named, because it is actually built from collected driftwood.*

Patio restaurants from odd pieces of lumber, and furnished them with a delightful mix of valuable and worthless items.

In the inn you find stained glass windows, priceless antiques, and bells from a Mexican mission. Waldo loved bells, and they are everywhere throughout the inn's eclectic decor. Sexton had mastodon bones and silver coins inlaid in the concrete work. This eccentric character even acquired valuable art when the huge mansions of the rich were sold off during the Depression, and The Patio is furnished with many items acquired in a Palm Beach estate auction. Ralph

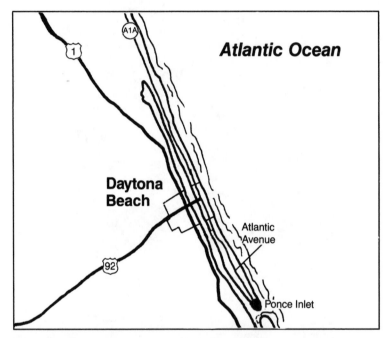

Sexton said of his father, "He looked at life a little differently, and collected junk. He loved things that people threw away."

## DAYTONA BEACH–PONCE INLET LIGHTHOUSE

*Atlantic Ave. to Ponce Inlet, 15 miles*

Just when you think the hotels and resorts of the main street of Daytona will never end, you finally arrive at a super little getaway: the Ponce de Leon Inlet Lighthouse. This magnificent old red tower is the second-tallest lighthouse on the eastern seaboard and the tallest in the United States still accessible to the public.

*Lighthouse fans will love Ponce de Leon Lighthouse. It's the tallest in the U.S. still open to the public.* Photo courtesy of the Ponce de Leon Lighthouse Preservation Association, Inc.

Night after night since 1887 this massive sentinel of brick and granite has flashed its warning to seamen. The beacon flashes every 10 seconds and can be seen for 16 nautical miles. The light went out in 1970 because the government decided the maintenance was too costly. Finally, after years of negotiation and restoration, the Coast Guard relit the navigational beacon in December, 1982. The entire property and outbuildings are maintained and operated by the Ponce de Leon Inlet Lighthouse Preservation Association.

You are welcome to climb the 203 steps spiraling to the top of the 175-foot lighthouse for a view of the inlet, New Smyrna Beach, and surrounding area. You can visualize the days of the blue-uniformed lighthouse keeper checking his oil supply and slowly climbing the tower to check his lens. The original lens built in Paris in 1863 has been replaced, but you can see the French lens in one of the museums.

Just across from the lighthouse is the Lighthouse Landing Restaurant. The menu is seafood, and the grouper sandwich is just superb. An entire fishing boat has been hauled inside and converted into a bar, and the local pelicans hang out at the docks.

Another spot you won't find loaded down with tourists is Sugar Mill Gardens in Port Orange, 8 miles south of Daytona Beach. Parts of a sugar mill built more than 300 years ago are still standing, looking like the perfect setting for errant ghosts. Indians burned the plantation, but enough is left to get a clear idea of the sugar industry in Florida centuries ago.

Stroll down the Dinosaur Trail and have a few giggles at the silly cement replicas of the "terrible lizards" that lived here before the Seminoles ever evolved.

## DAYTONA BEACH–CASSADAGA–DE LEON SPRINGS

*I-4, Daytona Beach to Cassadaga, 20 miles*

*US 17, Cassadaga to De Leon Springs, 14 miles*

*US 17, De Leon Springs to Barberville, 6 miles*

*SH 40, Barberville to Daytona Beach (via SH A1A or US 1), 27 miles*

*Total, 67 miles*

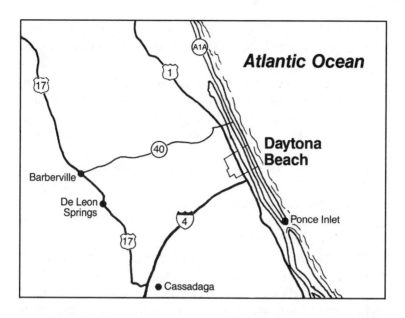

*Visit Florida's "other world." Of Cassadaga's 300 residents, 170 are psychics.*

The minute you enter the town limits of Cassadaga you know this place is definitely different. A little New England village seems right at home among the pines and palm trees of Central Florida. Picket fences, neat white cottages of 1880s vintage, an ancient hotel, one filling station, and a bookstore make up Cassadaga.

But there's more to Cassadaga than just a tidy hamlet. This has been a one-profession town since 1875 with its major industry guided by voices from the spirit world. Cassadaga was founded by George P. Colby, an early Spiritualist from New York in search of land and religious freedom. He was guided, so the story goes, by three spirits named The Philosopher, The Unknown, and Seneca. When Colby arrived at Cassadaga, it was sort of a Brigham Young "this is the place" revelation, and he founded the Southern Cassadaga Spiritualist Camp.

The followers of Spiritualism embrace the truths of all faiths. They believe in Jesus, Buddha, Zoroaster; everybody who was somebody in the world's great religions. To hang out a shingle and practice as a medium, a candidate has to undergo rigorous training and testing, and then he is licensed by the spiritual community. About 170 of the 300 residents of Cassadaga are involved in the occult.

Even if you don't believe in the world beyond, a trip to Cassadaga is a real experience. The most hardened of cynics are quick to admit there is a definite aura hanging over the town. Stroll down to Spirit Pond, then by the Healing Tree Park and Medium Walk. Or, just take a slow drive through the town and read the names on the mailboxes. You'll find "Reverend," "Sister," and "Dr." before the names of each resident. Most visitors find Cassadaga's atmosphere peaceful, serene, and very restful.

If you decide to have a reading, just go to The Book Store and inquire who is giving readings that day. Then drive or walk by their homes until the "vibes" lead you to the one you feel comfortable with. You may pick a medium who will put you in contact with the beyond, or perhaps a healer to help you with mental or physical pain. One of the best I found was a young man who was a palmist. Don't expect gypsies, crystal balls, or hocus-pocus. All of the spiritualists look more like they live in Mayberry on *The Andy Griffith Show* than some weird character from *The Twilight Zone.* Another medium I liked very much wore polyester and sounded like my grandmother.

Spiritualists do not deal in doom and gloom. Their approaches to you and your future are positive and can be full of good advice, with insights into your personality that you might well heed.

Weekly Spiritualist church services are held at the Colby Memorial Temple, and special seminars are conducted throughout the year. Healing services are also part of the church. For a schedule of programs and lectures and the history of Cassadaga, write: Southern Cassadaga Spiritualist Camp, Box 319, Cassadaga, FL 32706. The restored and charming Cassadaga Hotel is open for guests.

De Leon Springs State Park is actually the kind of Tom Sawyer place that Disney World spends a fortune to create. Its ancient Spanish Sugar Mill used spring power to crush the sugar cane, and John James Audubon commented on this great spring in 1832 with:

"This spring presents a circular basin having
a diameter of about sixty feet, from the centre of
which the water is thrown up with great
force. . . . The water is of a dark colour, but so
impregnated with sulphur, that it emits an odour
which to me was highly nauseous."

In the late 1800s tourists loved that odor which made Audubon highly nauseous, and the spring was billed as the Fountain of Youth. The mineral content has decreased in recent years and Audubon's "nauseous odour" has disappeared. However, the constant 76-degree water is still thought to have therapeutic value, and the pool is a refreshing swim.

But, De Leon Springs is a Florida "must" anytime of year. In the rustic mill is quite a unique restaurant. After you seat yourself at a table with a metal rectangle in the center, a cute young waitress instructs you to, ''Plug in your griddle, and I'll bring your batter.'' She soon arrives with pancake batter, (wholewheat and plain), eggs, raw bacon, cold ham, and whole-grain bread for French toast. Then you are on your own for breakfast. If your pancakes stick to the griddle, you should have put margarine down first, or cooked your ham and bacon first. Lumpy, sticky, raw, or just perfect, it's a great way to have breakfast. Ask for fresh blueberries and bananas to add to your batter. Get there at 9 am when the Mill opens. The secret is out about De Leon Springs and its pancakes, so you may have a wait. It is not easy to watch all that browning batter when your tummy is empty.

There are several other interesting state parks in the area. Blue Springs (2 miles west of Orange City off US 17) is more than a scenic area for canoeing and swimming. It is a place that plays a vital role in the survival of Florida's endangered manatees. These large mammals gather each winter in Blue Spring Run where the year-round 72-degree temperature of the spring run offers a refuge from the colder water of the St. Johns River. Manatees may be seen here from November through March.

Hontoon Island is 6 miles west of DeLand off SH 44. It is accessible only by private boat or a ferry which operates free of charge from 9 am until one hour before sundown. A replica of a Timucan Indian totem pole stands on the ceremonial grounds. Hontoon borders the St. Johns River, so you can watch a boat show all day. Or, better yet, rent your own houseboat at the Hontoon Landing Marina in DeLand (800-458-2474) and explore at your own pace. Those big stick nests you see are osprey nests. Don't worry, they are not as fragile as they look.

# SOUTHWEST FLORIDA

Thomas Alva Edison once wrote, "There is only one Fort Myers and 90 million people are going to find it out." Edison was a brilliant inventor, and he was a fairly accurate forecaster of things to come. Fort Myers may not have a population of 90 million just yet, but it is one of the fastest growing areas of Florida. Yet, you can still discover a few uninhabited islands and out-of-the-way beaches, wildlife sanctuaries, nature trails, and private coves.

One of the busiest highways in Florida is US 41, or the Tamiami Trail from Tampa to Miami. From Tampa to Marco Island both sides of the highway are lined with shopping centers and fast-food chains. If time is important, don't even think of driving US 41. Take I-75 and learn to love the fast lane of the interstate. From Naples east, I-75 is called Alligator Alley, and you can count on a very straight road and very flat scenery.

John Gaspar, the dreaded 18th century pirate, was rumored to have made men walk the plank in these Gulf Coast waters, and Captiva Island is supposedly the burial place of the pirate's booty. Don't spend your vacation searching for buried treasure, however. Many others have sifted these sands and never found a single doubloon. Just settle for lovely seashells.

Three men who did find gold here were Thomas Alva Edison, George Firestone, and Henry Ford. They collaborated to refine a silly contraption that Ford called the automobile. They also founded the Edison Botanical Research Company to find a new source of rubber for the United States. A set of tires was actually made from that weed cursed by hayfever sufferers, the goldenrod, and used on Edison's own Model T Ford.

It wasn't until the late 1800s that the southwest part of Florida began to bask in its own sunshine and enjoy its role as a world-class resort destination. Naturally, the millionaires came first, looking for the ultimate retreat, but you don't have to have a big bank account anymore to enjoy a special place in this special part of the Sunshine State.

## FORT MYERS

On the banks of the Caloosahatchee River, Fort Myers is best known as the beloved winter home of Thomas Alva Edison. At 38, Edison was a widower and seriously ill. Doctors told him he must seek a warm healthy climate, which he found in Florida, and thus lived a happy productive life until age 84. A visit to the home of this incredible genius is a must. Highlights of the conducted tour include Florida's first modern swimming pool, built by Edison and reinforced with bamboo, exotic gardens with the largest banyan tree in North America, the chemical laboratory where Edison experimented with goldenrod weeds as a source of rubber, and finally the Edison Museum. It may come as a surprise to learn that Edison only created one truly original invention— the phonograph. A strip of tinfoil five inches wide and 18 inches long—the world's first record—still plays ''Mary had a Little Lamb." The light bulb, motion pictures, and so on were Edison's improvements on earlier inventions. Edison's good friend Henry Ford had a home next door. Ford gave Edison a "tin lizzie" that Edison would never replace. So, Ford would just add every new automobile improvement to Edison's Model T, which is in the museum. The Henry Ford home, Mangoes, has been restored and is open to the public.

An institution in Southwest Florida for more than 40 years is The Shell Factory on US 41 in North Fort Myers. You can't miss the billboards. Shoppers will love 65,500 square feet of gift items from around the world, plus the "world's largest collection of rare shells, corals, sponges, and fossils from the seven seas."

## FORT MYERS–CAPTIVA ISLAND–SANIBEL ISLAND

*Toll causeway, 15 miles*

Just over the causeway from Fort Myers are the shrimp-shaped Sanibel and Captiva Islands. Visitors here all suffer from the disease called the "Sanibel stoop," and it is contacted by bending over to pick up the incredible variety of shells on the sparkling beaches. This is truly one of the few places in the world where one could make a fairly decent living guiding people to secluded beaches for the shelling. From Sanibel and Captiva, boats depart for sandbars like Johnson Shoals off the Cayo Costa State Preserve, another sheller's paradise. The best time for beachcombing is a low tide during the winter.

The 1884 Sanibel Lighthouse on the southern tip of the island is one of the most photographed sites in the area.

Located on the road to Captiva, north of the Sanibel Causeway, is the 5,030 acre J. N. "Ding" Darling National Wildlife Refuge. "Ding" was the nickname of Jay Norwood Darling, one of the pioneers of conservation. "Ding" made a living as a political cartoonist, and he did so well that he

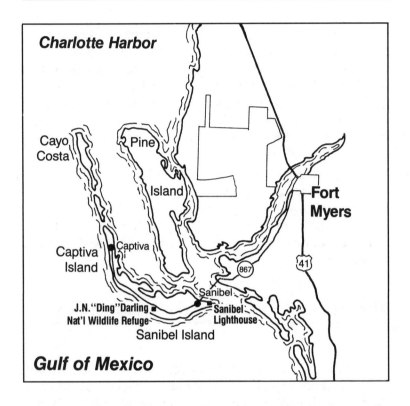

won the Pulitzer Prize in 1923 and again in 1942. One of "Ding's" most important contributions to wildlife was the initiation in 1934 of the Migratory Bird Hunting Stamp or "Duck Stamp" program. He designed the first stamp, and every year a new stamp is issued. The proceeds of these stamps continue to purchase wetlands for wildlife refuges.

The best time to enjoy the refuge is early in the morning, and the park is open from sunrise to sunset. The birds really do live by the old axiom, "The early bird catches the worm." So, to really enjoy the wildlife looking for its breakfast, you had best get there early, too. A highlight is the sight of crimson-winged roseate spoonbills coming and going in formation flight. Bring your binoculars and drive slowly. Walk as many trails as possible, and *take mosquito repellent.* The brochure at the Visitor's Center is invaluable.

There have been 291 species of birds, more than 50 types of reptiles and amphibians, and at least 32 different mammals recorded in the refuge.

## A WORD ABOUT ALLIGATORS

Florida loves its alligators, and you will see alligator logos all over the state on different businesses. This is an ugly critter and extremely dangerous if provoked. Its name comes from the Spanish *el lagarto* meaning "the lizard." The alligator's survival record is impressive, and it has been around a long time, about 250 million years. These direct descendants of dinosaurs look much the same as they did 35 million years ago, except perhaps a bit smaller.

Alligators catch their prey in powerful jaws and either crush or drown their victim. Remember, an alligator is not very smart and cannot distinguish the difference between the food offered him and the arm that holds out the tidbit. In other words, *don't feed the alligators.* Feeding an alligator trains it to approach humans and creates a life-threatening situation—especially for children and pets. In Florida, feeding alligators is a criminal act punishable by fines and/or imprisonment.

Sanibel prides itself on its protection of wildlife. Please only take two live shell specimens when out shelling. Sand dollars, sea stars, and sea urchins are protected and violators are subject to a $500 fine and 60 days in jail for a *first* offense. Snakes are protected, and it is illegal to kill any of them. Do not feed the racoons and don't disturb the turtles and tortoises. Drive slowly on the island, especially at night. Road kills are unnecessary.

Private homes line the main road down the islands, and much of the beach is hidden from drivers. You can tell that the owners aren't standing in any welfare line. In fact, every place on the islands reeks of money—big money. Charming shops, select little boutiques, big resorts, and lush golf courses are almost more noticeable than the beaches.

A wonderful touch of "Old Florida" is still found at the delightful 'Tween-Waters Inn on Captiva Island (800-282-7560 in Florida or 800-223-5865 nationwide). The charm of the inn dating from the 1920s mingles perfectly with today's modern conveniences. Its Old Captiva House restaurant has been an island favorite for over 50 years, and the full service resort offers every activity you could ever dream of wanting to do. "Ding" Darling and his wife spent their winters here.

Another unique dining experience is the Bubble Room Restaurant at 15001 Captiva Road. Talk about funky, art deco, silly, clever, amusing, and good food—and you have the Bubble Room. Every kind of trash and treasure imaginable has gone into the clever decor of this funky eatery.

At Channel Marker 60 in the Intracoastal Waterway, accessible only by boat, lies Cabbage Key. Built atop an ancient Indian shell mound, this cozy inn was constructed by novelist Mary Roberts Rinehart in 1938. Walls of the dining room and bar are covered with autographed dollar bills placed here by visitors. Jimmy Buffett had Cabbage Key in mind when he wrote his hit song "Cheeseburger in Paradise," and his autographed bill has a place of honor behind the bar. Non-boat-owners can take a regularly scheduled cruise via Island Fantasy Cruises in Punta Gorda (813-639-0969).

You can bunk overnight at the inn and dinner is served on a huge screened porch surrounded by a wonderful lighted jungle of ancient trees. Here is romance!

## FORT MYERS–PORT CHARLOTTE–BOCA GRANDE

*US 41 to Port Charlotte, 26 miles*

*SH 776 and County Road 771 to Boca Grande, 23 miles*

*Total miles, 49*

## ALTERNATE

*Babcock Wilderness Adventures*
*SH 74, Punta Gorda to Babcock, 20 miles*

At Port Charlotte and Punta Gorda the pace is a bit slower than in Tampa and Fort Myers. Ponce de Leon Park commemorates the landing place of the father of Florida. It was here that Ponce was fatally wounded while trying to establish a settlement. Cross a toll bridge ($3.25) at Placida to Gasparilla Island and Boca Grande. Boca Grande is another place in Florida where absolutely no one is poor. Secluded mansions worth millions are hidden behind massive gates,

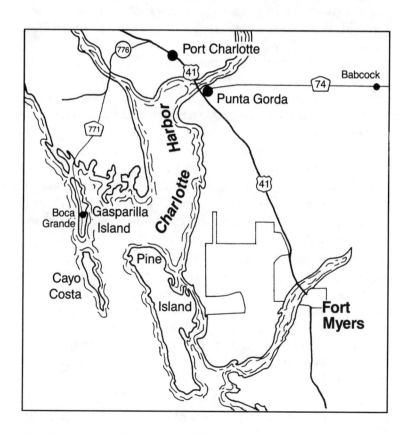

and even the tiny village of Boca Grande offers little more than a post office, Fugate's General Store, and the old Gasparilla Inn. At Fugate's you can buy toothpaste or a designer gown. One resident bought her dress for the presidential inaugural ball at Fugate's. The library, however, is not your usual small-town library. The courtyards have pools, sculptures of flamingos, and Henry Francis Du Pont's shell collection. The library has 15,000 books (about 25 for every resident) and a very hefty endowment.

If you try to book a room at the Gasparilla Inn (813-964-2201) during the winter, chances are slim to none that you will get a reservation. This is the high season for the wealthy, and the rooms and cottages that offer a bit of yesteryear are jammed. This huge, yellow clapboard hotel has changed little since the 1900s, and some of the rooms are as spartan as they were back then—not even air conditioned! Rooms do not have television, and the soap is definitely not French milled, but unimpressive Ivory. For these plain accommodations, you will pay up to $300 a night, but you'll have the chance to rub shoulders with the very rich.

Boca Grande Lighthouse Park is at the tip of the island where the 1890s lighthouse overlooks Boca Grande Pass. During tarpon season, April through July, the pass is crammed and jammed with tarpon fishermen. Also during tarpon season, the Gasparilla Inn unbends enough to permit men to forgo coats and ties for dinner.

Enjoy the excitement of a true wilderness adventure: take a swamp buggy ride through the deep woods and murky swamps of Telegraph Cypress Swamp with its thickets of slash pines, palmettos, sabal palms, cabbage palms, and resurrection ferns. Your guide, "Hunter" Richard, delivers a nonstop commentary on the flora and fauna of this primeval swamp. Listen up and you'll learn a great deal about Florida's animals and plants.

What's a good swamp without alligators? You'll see plenty of them in this swamp, but you may have to look carefully for the eyes, ears, and nose above the top of the water. Gators

*In Florida, the horse and buggy has been replaced by the swamp buggy.*

have a way of blending in with their territory so well that it takes an experienced eye to spot them. "Hunter" Richard will do the distress call of an alligator for you, and the water will come alive with slashing tails. Tannic acid keeps the swamp water murky and dark, but it is actually quite clean.

Birds abound in this wilderness and snowy white egrets and herons stand on stilt legs searching the water for fat bugs and careless fish.

"Hunter" Richard defends the snakes and points out they are the swamp's "good guys." Mice and rats are the most destructive of animals, and snakes keep them under control. You will also get to see a rare and endangered Florida panther, but it is in a pen and has been raised as a pet. This panther species is a victim of lost habitat and trophy hunters.

Babcock Wilderness Adventure is great fun, but you must have a reservation in advance. Call 813-639-4488 before you go to reserve a place on the swamp buggy.

## FORT MYERS–NAPLES–EVERGLADES CITY

*US 41, 73 miles*

ALTERNATE

*Corkscrew Swamp, 20 miles*

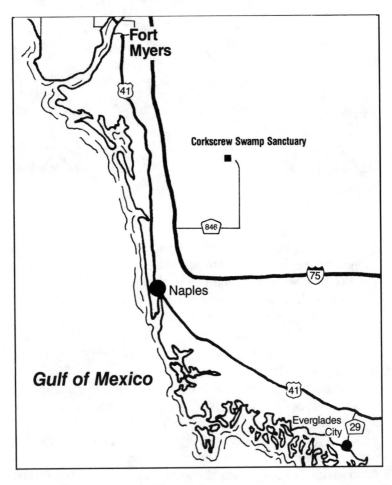

On your way down to Naples, pull off for a few minutes at the Koreshan State Historic Site. You have to wander down the trail for a view of the eight remaining buildings of a strange religious sect that practiced equal rights for women long before the concept was popular.

Koreshans lived by the Golden Rule, by doing unto others as you would have them do unto you, and they had a communal lifestyle that included shared ownership of property. The Koreshan Unity was established in the 1890s by Dr. Cyrus Read Teed, a Union Army Medical Corps veteran. Teed was inspired by a vision or "great illumination," which instructed him to change his name to Koresh, meaning Cyrus in Hebrew. He was instructed to move his followers to southwest Florida, where they would build a city covering 300 miles with 30-foot-wide streets and house 10 million people. Even at the peak of its popularity, Koreshan missed its population goal by 9,999,800.

An interesting, one-of-a-kind globe on the site illustrates the Koreshan belief that man resides on the inside surface of the earth, gazing at the solar system within.

Naples began like many Florida coast towns as nothing but dune grass, mangroves, and ragged palmettos harboring clouds of vicious mosquitoes. But this tiny fishing village, accessible only by boat, stood firm against the onslaught of storms, hurricanes, and hordes of biting insects.

By 1926, Barron G. Collier brought his railroad to Collier County and the world arrived in Naples. Today, Naples boasts more millionaires than any other town of its size in Florida. If your budget is not in the class with The Ritz Carlton on Vanderbilt Beach while visiting Naples, try the charming bed and breakfast, Inn by the Sea (813-649-4124). The Inn is just 700 feet from the Gulf of Mexico in a quiet residential neighborhood of quaint affluent cottages. Built in 1937, the Inn by the Sea is on the National Register of Historic Places.

While in Naples, take a riverboat cruise aboard the paddlewheeler *Rosie O'Shea* or ride to the posh shops of Third Street in a horse-drawn carriage. Stroll the 1,000-foot Naples Fishing Pier, take a trolley ride through town, or play golf. Naples claims to be the "Golf Capital of the World" with more golf courses per capita than anywhere else in the nation. Since nearly everything in Naples is truly elegant and caters to the affluent set, the Collier Automotive Museum at 2500 South Horseshoe Drive has on display the first Ferrari ever imported in the U. S., a 1919 Hispano-Suiza, a Bugatti, Gary Cooper's Deusenberg, and a 1913 Peugeot— the only one in the world.

*A 1928 Hispano-Suiza H6C "Boulogne" is among the permanent collection of classic and sports racing cars displayed at Collier Automotive Museum.* Photo courtesy of Collier Automotive Museum.

Visit Jungle Larry's Safari and Caribbean Gardens on US 41 at Alligator Alley. More than 50 years ago, world-famous botanist Dr. Henry Nehrling came to Naples and planted thousands of exotic trees and vines. Later, Julius Fleishmann added rare waterfowl to the gardens. In September of 1969, TV's zoologist and entertainer "Jungle Larry" Lawrence Tetzlaff turned the 200-acre complex into an exotic animal retreat.

Talk with a tiglon (half tiger, half lion), chat with a chimp, listen to a leopard, and eavesdrop on an elephant. Watch the big graceful cats perform their tricks, stroll through 52 acres of tropical gardens, take the kids to the petting zoo, and browse the gift shop.

Just south of Naples, detour down SH 951 to Marco Island. Named by the Spanish for St. Mark, it is hard to visualize that this island of posh condos and resorts was once a real hideaway. Yet, you can still enjoy fine dining in the oldest building on the island—the legendary Marco Island Inn located at Old Marco Village. Built with materials brought in by schooner, the 100-year-old inn is filled with fascinating treasures including the cranberry glass chandelier with its 2,000 prisms. And to think, in 1883 the inn advertised its rooms for $1 a day, and you had to furnish your own meat. By 1896, the owner, Captain Bill Collier, had completed his hotel with twenty rooms and one bathroom. This one bathroom was a two-story outhouse reported by Ripley in his "Believe it or Not." To see the island, Marco features a trio of trolleys, and all will take you on a tour of little-known sites as well as the ones with the high profiles.

Nature lovers will thoroughly enjoy the Rookery Bay National Estuarine Research Reserve with its half-mile elevated boardwalk. Ten miles from Marco is the Collier-Seminole State Park with its Royal Palm Hammock Nature Trail which takes you through a tropical hardwood hammock.

Everglades City is the starting point for numerous boat tours of the famous Everglades. The only tours allowed in the National Park Gulf Coast are the Everglades National Park Boat Tours, Inc. (800-445-7724 in Florida, or 800-233-1821 nationwide). You will cruise through the heart of the Ten Thousand Islands, the largest mangrove forest in the world. Frequently seen are ospreys, bald eagles, roseate spoonbills, manatees, dolphins, and turtles.

Numerous outfits offer airboat tours, swamp buggy rides, and alligator farms. One of the oldest is Wooten's Everglades Tours (813-695-2781).

---

### A WORD ON PELICANS

One of the most common feathered friends of Florida's waters is the Brown Pelican. For a while this comical bird was extinct in Louisiana, where it is the state bird, and highly endangered in Texas. But, in the warm blue waters of Florida, you will see thousands of these gregarious creatures. So beautiful in flight, the pelican waddles on shore like a fat awkward clown.

It is illegal to touch a wild bird, but there are exceptions. Karen Yuskaitis, on Smokehouse Creek, treats from one to three injured pelicans a day. Karen works in close cooperation with the Nature Conservancy to care for the birds until they can be returned to the wild. Birds that are so badly crippled they can never survive in the wild are given a permanent home. Most birds are injured by careless fishermen and boaters, and Karen begs sportsmen to please be aware of the plight of these wonderful pelicans.

---

About four miles east of Everglades City is Ochopee, the site of the nation's smallest post office. Tall and broad folks, beware! It's only 8 feet 4 inches by 7 feet 3 inches.

Return to Fort Myers via SH 49 to Immokalee, home of the third largest farmer's market in Florida. You are also only 14 miles from Corkscrew Swamp Sanctuary on County Road 846.

### CORKSCREW SWAMP SANCTUARY

*I-75, Exit 17 to County Road 846, 15 miles*

The National Audubon Society's Corkscrew Swamp Sanctuary contains one of the largest stands of mature bald cypress trees in the nation. Many of these towering giants are nearly 500 years old and shelter a lush swamp that was once deemed impenetrable. Yet, in the mid-fifties, even this

*No, it's not an outhouse . . . it's a U.S. Post Office.*

inaccessible wilderness was threatened with logging, drainage, and civilization. The loss of wildlife would have been heartrending to nature lovers. Luckily, the race to save this special place in nature was won, and the National Audubon Society accepted the responsibility for managing the area. More than a mile of boardwalk was built so that visitors could leisurely stroll this magnificent area—which someone characterized as being one million years from Miami.

Be sure to pick up the self-guided tour booklet that explains in detail the flora and fauna of the sanctuary. Amazingly, you do not need mosquito repellent on the trail. The balance of nature is so perfect that the dreaded Florida mosquitoes are not bothersome. This is not a place to feed wildlife, and you will find no captive animals on display. Otters may romp and play on the boardwalk or remain hidden. Bobcats will know you are here, but you will never see one. Alligators may or may not make their presence known, and between November and March wood storks may be nesting.

Birdwatchers come to Corkscrew mainly to study the wood storks. Sad to say, wood stork populations are in such a rapid rate of decline due to loss of habitat and food supply that in less than 20 years, the birds will probably be extinct. Massive drainage and development projects in southern Florida have so altered the surface water supply that the span of inundation has been drastically shortened. Yet, the sanctuary still has the largest colony of wood storks in the country.

Currently, the sanctuary encompasses 11,000 acres. But, no wilderness here can be secure because southern Florida is one of the country's fastest growing areas. Any major changes in the watershed would damage the entire ecosystem of the sanctuary. The Audubon Society needs your support, and you may contact them at 950 Third Avenue, New York, NY 10022.

# SOUTHEAST FLORIDA

Southeast Florida has it all. Big cities, rich cities, famous beaches, the mysterious Everglades, huge Lake Okeechobee, small towns, and the fun-filled Keys. Yet, all are in big trouble because of water. There just isn't enough to irrigate the farms, water the golf courses, fill the resort swimming pools, and keep the Everglades alive. Something will have to go, and chances are it will be the Everglades.

The inland part of southeast Florida revolves around the tremendous Lake Okeechobee, an Indian name for "big water." Florida's largest lake is 750 square miles and tamed by a system of dikes, pumping stations, spillways, and canals. The result is an agricultural paradise. Here are cowboys and Indians in real life, and both raise cattle and sugar cane.

Okeechobee's fate is a bone of contention between environmentalists and developers. The lake is slowly and surely drying up. The Everglades and south Florida's cities have been threatened by drought and excessive population growth, and industry and agriculture have been sucking Okeechobee dry.

Florida's southeast coast, called the Gold Coast, is lined with names synonymous with wealth: Palm Beach, West Palm Beach, Boca Raton, Miami Beach, and Coral Gables. Yet, Miami was only a fishing village on the edge of a gigantic swamp when it was incorporated in 1896. Railroad magnate Henry Flagler was skeptical about the future of Miami even as track was being laid into town.

But, long before the world ever heard of Flagler, the first white man in the area was a poor shipwrecked soul enslaved by the Tequesta Indians. He later wrote about a place the Indians called the "Lake of Mayaime," and historians speculate he meant Lake Okeechobee. Regardless, somehow, Mayaime evolved into Miami, the Tequesta word for "sweet water."

One of the first snowbirds to arrive in Miami was Julia Tuttle, who convinced Flagler to extend the railroad to Biscayne Bay. Smart Julia sent Flagler a bouquet of orange blossoms in the middle of winter, and smart Flagler sent Julia his railroad. Land speculation was rampant, but the 1926 hurricane and then the Great Depression ended Miami's first growth phase.

For years, Miami Beach was the average American's dream vacation, but in the '70s Walt Disney World became the dream vacation. Miami Beach suffered when its faithful worshipers deserted its shores. Fortunately, a renaissance is taking place in the Art Deco District on Miami Beach, and once again this is becoming an "in" spot in Miami.

A few "Old Florida" attractions have survived in spite of Disney World, and it is refreshing to discover them alive and well, although not too easy to find. If Miami is your home base, consider the Cavalier Hotel and Cabana Club. Built in 1936 and carefully restored, the Cavalier is situated on the ocean in the Art Deco National Historic District (305-534-2135). Another delightful spot is the Bay Harbor Inn on the banks of Indian Creek just a splash away from civilization and the exclusive shops of Bal Harbour. Dining on the waterfront terrace, high tea in The Gallery, rooms right on the waterway . . . it's paradise (305-868-4141).

Coral Gables was the brainchild of George Merrick and touted by silver-tongued William Jennings Bryan. The country's first planned community boasted regal entrance gates, pools, hotels, golf courses, zoned business districts, and alluring lots. Coral Gables still retains its charm, and you can soak up this opulent ambiance at the 1926 Hotel Place St. Michael (305-444-1666). No two rooms are alike and all are filled with antiques, flowers, and paintings. The restaurant and lounge are superb.

## OUT AND AROUND MIAMI

For a map showing the following sites in detail, contact the Greater Miami Convention and Visitors Bureau at 305-573-4300 and ask for: Official Map: Miami, Fort Lauderdale, West Palm Beach, Key West.

### CORAL CASTLE

*SW 288 St. at US 1 or take the Turnpike (SH 821) to Homestead AFB exit and follow signs.*

What do most jilted lovers do? They go out and find another lover, but that's not what Ed L. (as he called himself) did. In 1923, Ed Leedskalnin's fiancee threw him over, and Ed L. left Latvia for a fresh start in Florida. Instead of searching for another fiancee, however, Ed L. searched for rocks, coral rocks. For 20 years Ed L. mined, hauled, and carved tons of coral. Working totally alone with hoists and pulleys made from Model-T parts, he created Coral Castle from 1,110 tons of rock. Ed L., who only weighed 100 pounds, never revealed his methods of construction. Baffled engineers have compared Coral Castle's construction to

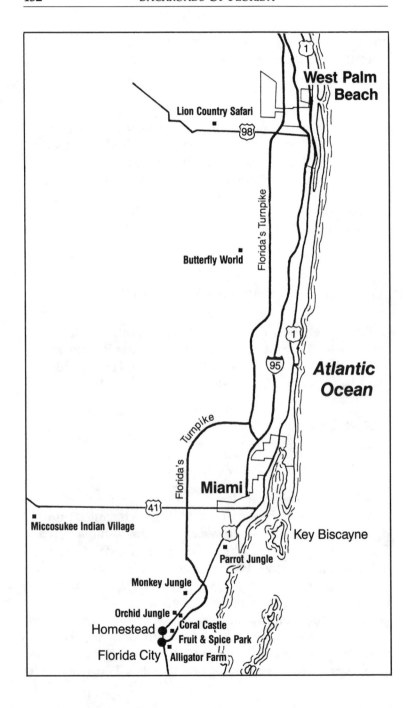

Stonehenge and the Great Pyramids. When he died in 1951, Ed L. took his secret to the grave.

The wall around the castle courtyard is composed of huge coral stones, the largest weighing 29 tons. On the north wall is the Polaris telescope which is perfectly focused on the North Star and weighs 30 tons. His sundial records the hours between 9 a.m. and 4 p.m. Eastern Standard Time—the hours he believed a man should work.

*Ed Leedskalnin built his fiancée a coral castle, but she ditched him anyway.*

Ed also believed every man's home was his castle and every castle should have a throne. Ed's throne weighs 5,000 pounds and actually rocks gently back and forth. He loved tables, and his State of Florida Table was carved in the exact shape and correct proportions of the state and surrounded by 10 chairs. Lake Okeechobee is the finger bowl.

Surrounded by his beloved fountains, playgrounds, gates, chairs, and other coral creations, Ed L. lived in the tiny room of his two-story tower. A few boards hang from the ceiling as his bed and not much else makes up his spartan quarters. The monument to Ed L.'s genius is the Nine-ton Gate. With the slightest touch of a finger, a gate 80 inches wide, 92 inches tall, and 21 inches thick fits within a quarter of an inch of the walls on both sides.

When Coral Castle was sold after Ed L.'s death, $3500 was found in $100 bills—his life savings.

## ORCHID JUNGLE

*From Miami follow US 1 to 26715 SW 157th Ave. in Homestead*

Orchids grow all over the world and have adapted to every environment except Antarctica. More than 30,000 species of orchids have been able to carve out successful niches in thin mountain air, steamy tropical jungles, and arid wastelands. The Fennell family have been growing orchids since 1888. Starting in Kentucky, the Fennells moved to Florida in 1922 and now operate a fourth generation business with the largest collection of orchid varieties in the United States.

Your self-guided tour through Orchid Jungle allows you to spend as much time as you like admiring these rare and delicate plants. Actually, orchids are very hardy plants; they just look delicate. Most of the orchids growing in this lush jungle grow as epiphytes attached to trees. Look up to see them as you follow the path, but don't forget also to read the signs concerning the orchids and other unusual plants.

The tour ends in three main display houses with plants in full bloom. In the gift shop you can purchase many of the plants, complete with a booklet on the care and feeding of orchids. Fennell's even has an orchid help-line number (305-247-4824) for any problem you may have with this exciting hobby.

## MONKEY JUNGLE

*US 1, Florida Turnpike South or SH 27 to 14805 SW 216th Street, Miami*

Monkey Jungle is America's only habitat "where the humans are caged and the monkeys run wild." More than 50 years ago, Joseph DuMond, an inquisitive animal behaviorist, released six crab-eating macaques into the wilds of a dense South Florida hammock. He had no idea how his endeavors would later shape the attitudes of many zoologists. Ahead of his time, DuMond believed animals should be placed in their natural habitat, not confined to tiny cages.

During the Depression years, DuMond began charging a dime to curious visitors who had heard stories about the wild monkeys. There were no screened walkways separating the public from the monkeys, and these territorial primates viewed humans as a threat and aggressively defended their jungle home. DuMond could not cage his wild monkeys, so he caged his visitors instead.

The descendants of these Java monkeys now number more than 80. They are skilled skin divers in the wild and

*At Monkey Jungle, the people are in cages.*

will show off as they dive into a pool to receive fruit from the guides.

In the Asiatic Ape Compound, you'll see an orangutan family lounging among the trees. Highly endangered in Malaysia, this shaggy ape with ugly orange hair is among the most intelligent of the primates.

The world of the Amazonian Rainforest is home to more than 200 chattering shrieking monkeys. The squirrel monkey dominates the five other species of the rainforest because it has adapted successfully and reproduced well at Monkey Jungle.

Other exhibits include gibbons, guenons, Barbary apes, chimpanzees, colobus monkeys and owl monkeys. The tiny monkey with the fiery red fur around its face is the golden lion tamarin. Only several hundred remain in their native Brazil, and Monkey Jungle is proud to be part of an international effort to save the beautiful creature from extinction.

Monkey Jungle is an intimate glimpse into the life of primates—the drama of a remarkable society like no other in the animal kingdom.

## FRUIT & SPICE PARK

*Take US 1 or the Florida Turnpike to Coconut Palm Drive (SW 248 Street) and head east to 24801 SW 187th Avenue (Redlands Road) in Homestead, approximately 35 miles south of Miami.*

Established in 1944, the Fruit & Spice Park is a tropical paradise in the heart of the Redland Historic District. Surrounded by thousands of acres of tropical agriculture, the Park is the showcase for the south Florida agricultural community. More than 500 varieties of exotic fruits, herbs, spices, and nuts from throughout the world can be found in this lush 20-acre park.

The Redland Gourmet & Fruit Store is a fruit lover's delight with dried fruit, canned fruit, and fresh fruit in season. Wonderful spices, jams, and jellies line the shelves as well, plus teas, and unusual seeds for you to start your own exotic plant garden. You can try to grow a carambola (star fruit) tree from Malaysia which will produce up to 300 pounds of fruit per year. Sip a glass of cold fruit juice as you browse among the goodies offered, and the cookbooks for sale will tell you how to prepare your purchases.

Classes and workshops on tropical agriculture are held all year, and reservations are required for these as well as for tours (305-247-5727). A guidebook is available for your tour to help identify the plants. For those who want to join a "fruit safari" for botanists, students, growers, and gourmets led by the park's director, Chris Rollins, to the wilds of South America and Malaysia, write the park at 24801 SW 187 Ave., Homestead, FL 33031 for details.

All along SH 997 you will see U-Pick-Em signs for local orchards and berry farms. Also lining the road are fresh fruit and vegetable stands with produce just waiting for you to stop and shop. The granddaddy of fruitstands is Robert Is Here Fruit Stand at 19900 SW 344th Street in Homestead. Robert owns his own groves and sells Monstera Deliciosa, carambola, mamey, lychee, papaya, and mango, plus other fruit you've never heard of, and Robert's mom puts up jellies and preserves for sale. Drive up and get your wallet out: there's no way you can pass up these treats.

For serious growers, Farm Tours of Dade County are held December through April. Buses leave from the Farmers Market in Florida City (305-248-6798).

## JOHN HUDSON'S ALLIGATOR FARM

*SW 192nd Street, Florida City*

If there is one attraction Florida has in abundance, it's alligator farms. Most of the farms exist purely to make money off the tourists driving by, but John Hudson raises 'gators to make money off 'gators. Forget the gift shops and snack bars, all you will see here is a man in business selling alligator hides and meat.

Hudson started out trying to attract tourists, but now they are just a sideline. Finished alligator wallets run about $150 and belts for as much as $300. A good pair of shoes sells for more than $1,000. Meat wholesales at $7 a pound, so nothing is wasted on the reptile.

Hudson is a former Baptist preacher and still very much a man of God. Most of his workers are former alcoholics from the Home of Grace in Van Cleave, Mississippi, a Christian halfway house.

Lots of tourists stop at Hudson's, and the first thing you notice is the acrid aroma of alligators assailing your nostrils. Those beasts do have a distinctive odor, particularly when a large number are put in one pen. After a brief tour of the farm, and brief is enough unless you have a deep fascination for the breeding habits of alligators, take one of Hudson's airboat tours.

Stuff your ears full of cotton and roar off into the sawgrass and hammocks on an exciting ride. It really is fun, and the drivers have a great sense of humor as they give you lessons on wildlife in the Everglades. Don't worry, you really won't fall off into the jaws of lurking 'gators.


## PARROT JUNGLE AND GARDENS

*11000 SW 57th Avenue off US 1 south, Miami*

Florida is blessed with so many lovely gardens that a complete guidebook could be written just on this subject. One of the oldest is Parrot Jungle and Gardens. For more than 50 years this authentic Florida jungle has been a preserve for free-flying macaws, magnificent flamingos (as seen on TV's *Miami Vice*), rare parrots, and cockatoos.

Continuous shows throughout the day are staged in the Parrot Bowl Theater where Amazon parrots sing and talk, cockatoos roller-skate and ride scooters, and colorful macaws count and play cards. You can even hold these beautiful birds and have your picture taken.

*If you want to hear more than "Polly wants a cracker,"
listen to the chatter at Parrot Jungle.*

To add to the exotic scene, there are also giant tortoises, strutting peacocks, and prehistoric iguanas. And, what would a Florida garden be without its alligators, so you will find those as well. The Parrot Cafe serves snacks and cold drinks, and the gift shop is filled with souvenirs.

## BUTTERFLY WORLD

*Turn west off the Florida Turnpike on Sample Road to
Tradewinds Park, Coconut Creek*

How long does a butterfly live? This is the one question most asked at Butterfly World. And, it seems so sad that such beautiful creatures are lucky to survive in the wild for seven days. However, some species like the zebra can live for up to ten months.

Docents at Butterfly World get asked many questions about the gorgeous specimens in this unique setting. You will find not only a butterfly farm, but a pupa emerging area, a museum, and botanical and water gardens. This park is the first of its kind in the United States and the largest in the world with more than 3,000 butterflies representing as many as 80 different species from five continents.

Don't bring a butterfly net with you to Butterfly World. You don't need one. Here, they flutter around you like

*Butterfly World is not only the first of its kind in the United States, but the largest butterfly museum in the world.*

leaves and brush your shoulders and hair so slightly, you never know they are there. With no fear of humans, these gorgeous insects may think you are just another bright flower in their garden.

To have butterflies, you must have flowers. Most butterflies feed on a single kind of plant or require one specific plant on which to lay their eggs. In return, the butterflies pollinate the plants while feeding on their nectar. More than 10,000 plants in Butterfly World represent hundreds of different species, so here is also a treat for plant lovers. You will thrill to the arbor of passion vines covered with breathtaking blossoms just outside the museum. These blooms are the lifeline of the Heliconius butterflies.

Visitors can follow the life cycle of these delicate creatures from the egg to the final emergence of the butterfly from its pupa. In the breeding area, caterpillars shed their skins in public and change into pupae before your eyes. It is truly one of nature's miracles when the dull pupae and cocoons burst open for the emergence of a masterpiece of nature's handiwork.

## LION COUNTRY SAFARI

*18 miles off I-95 on Southern Blvd. (SH 80) west to entrance, West Palm Beach*

JAMBO! In Swahili, jambo means WELCOME! And, you are more than welcome at the nation's first drive-through "cageless" zoo which opened in 1967. So, take a drive on the wild side at Lion Country Safari. Put on your pith helmet, load up the camera, get a booklet describing the animals, and don't get out of the car.

Your first stop is Lake Nakaru, named for Kenya's soda lake that is famous for its flamingos. The flamingos here in Lion Country are from Peru and Chile and range from light pink to white in color. You will see the bright pink Caribbean flamingos at the Safari World Amusement Park. The color of the flamingo depends entirely on the amount of carotene in its diet. Carotene is found in some vegetables and most shellfish, so flamingos in captivity are usually fed diets of shrimp.

Meander on to the Great Plains where herds of bison roam, then to the most interesting part of Lion Country, the Gorongosa Reserve with its pride of lions. Lions love to sleep, particularly if the weather is hot and their tummies are full. Since these lions don't have to move a muscle for their daily fare, you can almost bet they will be lolling happily in the shade totally ignoring the cars driving by.

Most of the antelopes will be grazing on the Serengeti Plains. The handsome little blackbuck is from India, and the big lumbering eland, the largest of the antelopes, is native to Africa. You end your tour of Lion Country in Western Zimbabwe at Wankie National Park, home of the big guys—elephants, rhinos, and Cape buffalo. You are welcome to drive around Lion Country as many times as you wish for the price of one ticket.

Allow time for Safari World and see Monkey Island, the Petting Zoo, and the Nature Trail. You will enjoy a *Safari Queen* Cruise, a rest at the Snack Shop, and more. For a really wild night, camp at Lion Country's KOA Kampground and be serenaded to sleep by the roar of the lions, the whoops of the gibbons, an elephant trumpeting, and whatever else decides to grumble and groan before dawn.

## MICCOSUKEE INDIAN VILLAGE

*25 miles west of Miami on US 41 (305-223-8380)*

All of the Florida Indians trace their roots back to about 200 souls led into the wilderness by Chief Billy Bowlegs after the Seminole Wars of the 1850s. They disappeared into the marshes and refused to budge, and finally the mighty U. S. Government gave up and let them be.

This village culture center features a model of the kind of home these early Indian refugees lived in to escape the white man's world. You will see a cooking chickee, sleeping

*Check out one of Florida's largest Indian reservations. Here is alligator
wrestling at its best.*

chickee, and all sorts of chickees where the Indians demon-
strate beadwork and sewing. If you haven't guessed, a
chickee is a room.

And, all the tourists want to see the alligator wrestling.
An Indian jumps into a pit and finally gets a sleeping 'gator
to wake up. Then the two-footed wrestler drags the big
reptile to a sand pit and pries open its powerful jaws. The
snout is clamped between the wrestler's chest and chin, and
he rubs the 'gator's throat "to put it to sleep." Somehow,
you get the impression that the alligator has been set up to
lose the fight and go down for the count.

The restaurant and Information Center are across the
street. The food is definitely ho-hum, but the airboat rides
are definitely exhilarating!

Next to the Village is the Shark Valley entrance station to
the Everglades. In the winter, the park operates a tram ride
through the sawgrass and up to an observation tower. You
can also walk or bike the tram route.

## MIAMI–CLEWISTON–OKEECHOBEE

*US 27 to Clewiston, 99 miles*
*SH 78 to Okeechobee 34 miles*
*US 441, Okeechobee to West Palm Beach, 75 miles*
*I-95 to Miami, 64 miles*
*Total Miles, 272*

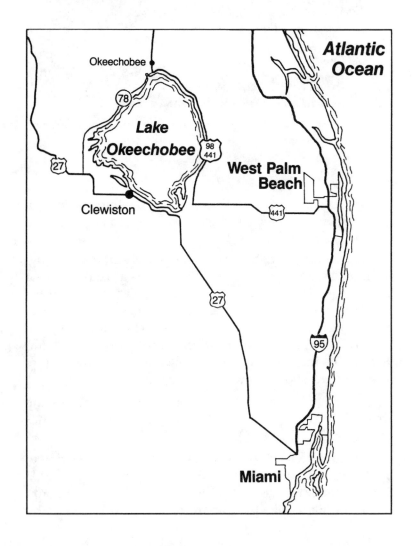

Lake Okeechobee is the second-largest freshwater lake within the boundaries of a single state. You won't see this mighty lake from US 27 as you drive from Belle Glade to Clewiston, because the 35-foot Hoover Dike obscures the view. It took 40 years to build this earthen dam, but when the hurricanes arrive, Okeechobee's waters stay where they belong. More than 2,400 people died in the 1928 hurricane floodwaters before Hoover Dike was constructed. On the environmental side of the coin, Hoover Dike blocks the essential flow of water needed to maintain the ecology of the Everglades.

The roadside scenery is less than exciting as it's miles and miles of sugarcane fields. Clewiston is headquarters for the U. S. Sugar Corporation, the south's largest sugar mill. To give you an idea of its size, 93 million gallons of blackstrap molasses are produced for cattle feed.

Clewiston is not a very old town; it was incorporated in 1932. Because of its reliance on the sugar industry, its motto is "The sweetest town in the U. S. A." Since 1938, the center of all social activity has been the Clewiston Inn. This grand old inn was built by the U. S. Sugar Corporation to house visiting dignitaries and executives of the company.

Queen Anne furniture and southern hospitality are part of the Clewiston Inn today, and you don't have to be famous or a company executive to be welcome (813-983-8151). Whatever you do, pause long enough to visit the bar at the Clewiston Inn to view the famous Mural of Wildlife in the Everglades by J. Clinton Sheperd of Palm Beach, now deceased. This huge canvas was hung on the walls in 1945 and valued at $40,000. A brochure will help you identify the wildlife in the mural.

Even if you wanted to, you can't miss the Old South Bar-B-Q Ranch in Clewiston. Flags wave (Confederate, of course), wagon wheels roll, stuffed cowboys aim their six-shooters, and tons of relics urge you to partake of real pit Bar-B-Q and catfish 'n hush puppies. Inside are more relics, lots of homey little quotes, friendly people, and good food.

Heading north on SH 78 you'll pass by the Calusa Lodge, a resort for hunters and fishermen. Okeechobee is the largest town on the north shore of the lake and a big agricultural center for vegetables grown in the muckland, as the fields are called in southern Florida. Naturally fishing is also important on this monster lake, and Okeechobee is the "Speckled Perch Capital of the World."

If you opt to head north up US 27 toward Palmdale, you'll find two hangovers from "Old Florida" that have survived sort of out in nowhere. A line of tree limbs beg you to visit Tom Gaskins' Cypress Knee Museum, so please stop. How can you resist Tom's signs reading "What's your cypress knee I. Q.?" and "The Jones have seen it twice."

Gaskins began collecting cypress knees in 1934 when he noticed their natural shapes resembled camels, wishbones, a brain, and whatever his active mind conjured up. On one side of the road is the museum with his favorites: Rudolph, Donald Duck, FDR, and even the Mona Lisa—all in cypress knees. Some figures may require a vivid imagination on your part, but you'll love Gaskins' little homilies that go with them.

On the other side of the road is the store, and you can also watch a video of how the knees are boiled for two hours, but none have been polished, sanded, or colored. Also, the

*Don't take home a seashell souvenir: buy a cypress knee instead.*

sap is very nutritious if you care to suck on a cypress knee. Everybody takes home Mickey T-shirts and seashells. Dare to be different, take back cypress knees.

On up US 27 is Gatorama. This roadside attraction is sort of low key, but let's face it—it's just another Florida alligator farm. There's no amusement park, just Patty's Gator Grill and a gift shop. If you stop, your car may be the only one in the lot.

## THE EVERGLADES

Some experts believe that in a few decades the Everglades will vanish forever. And, with the seas of grass will also disappear, from this southern tip of Florida, nearly 300 varieties of birds and 600 kinds of fish. Forty-five indigenous species of plants found nowhere else in the world will be lost forever.

Author of the book *River of Grass*, Marjory Stoneman Douglas said in 1989 at age 99, "If the Everglades go, then South Florida becomes a desert. The greatest threat isn't pollution, but the draining of land to accommodate the boom in one of the fastest growing states." Douglas' book was published in 1947 and is still in print.

It was also 1947 before Everglades National Park was established with 1.4 million acres, an area larger than the state of Delaware. Unlike many of America's national parks which take your breath away with their beauty and grandeur, the Everglades is truly what Stoneman said: a river of grass. Sawgrass stretches in all directions, broken only by occasional hammocks (high spots of land) of trees and clumps of mangroves.

Underneath the sawgrass is a slow moving river called Pa-hay-okee or "grassy waters" by the Indians. An early English surveyor called it "River Glades," but somehow "river" was later changed to "ever," creating its present perfect name.

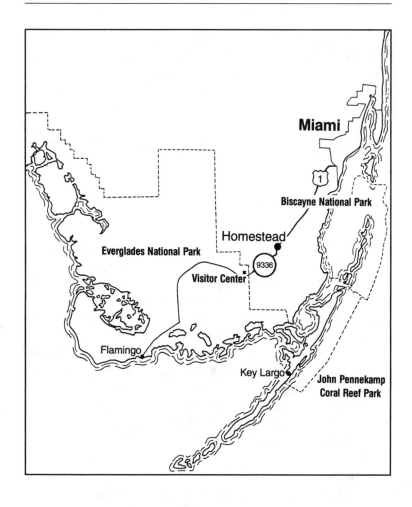

Man-made dikes and canals have changed the Everglades forever. Fields are flooded when the Everglades should be dry, and the flow of water curtailed when they should be wet. Much of the glades has been planted in sugar cane and vegetables, and cities of the Gold Coast have plugged into its aquifer. The delicate environment has been so altered that even the shortest drought can do incredible damage.

The Everglades took six million years, more or less, to form and yet in less than a century man has almost totally destroyed it. With 10,000 people a day moving into Florida, the future of the Glades looks bleak indeed.

Begin your expedition into this fascinating and unique part of the world at the Visitor Center on SH 9336. Or, for an advance course in Evergladology, write for the informative brochure to U. S. Department of Interior, Everglades National Park, P. O. Box 279, Homestead, FL 33030, or call (305-247-6211).

It is about 38 miles from the entrance of the park to Flamingo, and if you really want to experience the Everglades, plan to stay all day or even all year. But, no matter what time of year you go, *take mosquito repellent.* One of God's critters that is not on the endangered species list is the Florida mosquito.

All along the one paved road are fantastic nature trails. From cool rain forests to grassy prairies to mangrove clusters you will find rare plants and wildlife. Some trails are for paddling your canoe and lead deep into parts of the Everglades called the backcountry.

Flamingo is a great place to make your headquarters during your Everglades exploration. There you'll find a marina, camping, boat rentals, tour boats, and hiking and biking trails. They also sell mosquito repellent. Just be sure to file your plans with the ranger station. No kidding, even skilled sportsmen and locals have vanished—forever.

For those who prefer more creature comforts than a sleeping bag, the Flamingo Inn has 120 motel rooms, a restaurant, and bar. Just book with the Park Service well in advance.

Some of the wildlife treasures in the River of Grass are the roseate spoonbills, ospreys, brown pelicans, wood storks, bald eagles, anhingas, and the ever-popular alligators. These are easy to spot on your hikes. Chances of seeing the rare Florida panthers, crocodiles, and manatees are slim. There are only 26 known panthers in the Everglades and Big

Cypress. This state animal of Florida has three distinct characteristics: a whorl of hair in the middle of its back, a crook in the end of its tail, and irregular white flecks on its shoulders, neck, and head. Their biggest enemy is man's destruction of their habitat. Naturalists conduct hikes and canoe trips, so for more information, inquire at the Visitor Center.

Concern for protecting rookeries of herons, ibis, and other wading birds from commercial plume hunting and other human impact motivated the creation of Everglades National Park. Ironically, the park is now a refuge for people, too. Ultimately, places like the Everglades may be the last refuge—for all living things.

## BISCAYNE NATIONAL PARK

> *Take SW 137 Ave. from either US 1 or the Florida Turnpike, 25 miles south of Miami*
>
> *Contact: Capt. Ed Davidson*
>
> *P. O. Box 1270*
>
> *Homestead, FL 33030*
>
> *305-247-2400*

Biscayne National Park has 20 miles of precious reef and two charter boats. It also has Captain Ed Davidson, who challenged, denounced, and litigated to keep the condominiums at bay and helped preserve a precious bit of Florida.

Captain Ed looks almost like a boat bum in a handsome sort of way, but when he starts to talk about preservation, you know you are listening to a man that knows his business. It was Captain Ed's long and lengthy fight against a new subdivision called Port Bougainville that saved a last pristine part of the Florida ecosystem.

But, Captain Ed is not content with his one victory. He is still protesting the destruction of the Florida Keys by encroaching civilization. A tour on his boat is not just a look at a gorgeous coral reef, but also an education in how reefs must be preserved and what we can do. Snorkelers and scuba divers are briefed in detail on reef preservation before descending into the water.

Davidson explains that Biscayne National Park is blessed with its proliferation of giant, beautiful patch reefs, which occur nowhere else in the Keys. Because of pollution, the other patch reefs throughout the keys are stunted. Davidson's two boats are the only tour boats allowed at Biscayne. He points out that John Pennekamp Coral Reef Park, to the south ". . . has fifty charter boats and a million and a half visitors a year. Biscayne, with twenty miles of reef, has two charter boats. The reefs here are in much better shape and there are no crowds. This is what the rest of the Keys were like thirty years ago."

Davidson's two *Reef Rovers* draw only 30 inches of water and both are capable of venturing over reefs that most glass-bottomed boats would have to leave for the fish. Trips are scheduled every day of the year, and reservations are required. Just meeting Captain Ed is worth the trip.

There are no camping, restaurant, or motel facilities in the park. A new Hampton Inn is in nearby Florida City (305-247-8833).

# FLORIDA KEYS
# AND KEY WEST

The Overseas Highway, sometimes known by the more romantic name of "The Highway that Goes to the Sea," is a modern wonder. It is the "magic carpet" on which visitors cross countless coral and limestone islets on the way to that special world of the Florida Keys.

On May 15, 1513, adventurer Ponce de Leon and his fellow Spanish chronicler Antonio de Herrera sighted the Florida Keys. Herrera was not impressed and wrote, "To all this line of islands and rock islets they gave the name of *Los Martires* because, seen from a distance, the rocks as they rose to view appeared like men who were suffering: and the name remained fitting because of the many that have been lost there since."

In his search for the Fountain of Youth, de Leon passed on by *Los Martires*, but eventually settlers arrived and the native Indians, the Caloosa (or Calusa) died out. Farming was the main industry on those coral rocks, and productive groves of Key limes, tamarind, and breadfruit were common.

Pineapple fields flourished, and the Keys furnished canned pineapple to most of eastern North America.

Big Pine Key was the site of a thriving shark factory. Hides were skinned, salted down, and sent north to be processed into a tough leather called shagreen.

Another major industry at Islamorada and Key West was salvaging goods from ships that met their doom on nearby reefs. Legend has it that some ships were deliberately lured ashoal by greedy wreckers, and that ship captains and wreckers made deals whereby both made a nice return. Key West became the wealthiest city in the infant United States Republic from the booty of wrecked ships.

Today, you might see a different type of salvager at work. Sometimes dozens of bales of marijuana wash up on the shores of the Keys, and locals call it "square grouper." Once word gets out that a load had to be dropped at sea, the beaches fill up with potential rescuers. One T-shirt capitalized on the phenomenon with "Save The Bales."

Later in the Keys' history, fishermen found a good market for the high quality sponges harvested in these waters, and still later, cigar makers from Cuba established factories for hand-rolling cigars in Key West. When railroad tycoon Henry Flagler built his impossible "railroad to the sea," the Keys boomed with wealthy vacationers. A historical marker next to the Holiday Inn in Key West states, "At 9:43 a.m., January 22, 1912, 15,000 citizens of Key West, many of whom had never seen a train, stood here and watched the arrival of five cars carrying the Henry M. Flagler party . . ."

All of that glorious prosperity was short-lived, however, for The Great Depression arrived, and Key West went bankrupt. Yet, the Keys officials decided that their special spot still had the sea, the sun, and a benevolent winter climate. When the railroad began to suffer from storms and erosion of the track bed, the concept of a highway was born. Construction of the Overseas Highway was a formidable engineering feat. Following a trail originally blazed in 1912 with the Flagler railroad, the highway consists of a total of

113 miles of roadway and 42 oversea bridges leapfrogging from key to key. The famed Florida Keys Overseas Highway opened in 1938, but World War II dashed all prospects of tourist dollars.

The U. S. Navy salvaged Key West with a submarine base, and after the war shrimp were discovered—the Keys' now vital "pink gold." After the war, somewhat weatherbeaten and shabby, the Keys finally began to see the arrival of the long-awaited tourists.

The Conch Republic was born in 1982 when the U.S. Border Patrol set up a surprise roadblock just north of the Keys, trapping tourists in a 19-mile traffic jam. All pleas to abandon the roadblock were rejected, and the Keys faced a financial disaster. Stu Newman, owner of a public relations agency, suggested the crisis be turned into an opportunity. Newman suggested a mock secession. Key Westers seized the chance to have a great time, and they developed the spoof Conch Republic. In true Key West style, they celebrate the Conch Republic every year.

Unlike Ponce de Leon, today's visitors find their own special Fountain of Youth in the fun-loving Florida Keys.

## US 1, KEY LARGO TO KEY WEST

"The Highway that Goes to the Sea" underwent vast reconstruction during 1982 and you can drive easily from Miami to Key West in less than three hours. But, instead of three brief hours, take three leisurely days, for here is an ever-changing, challenging world of seas and lost wilderness that can only be savored in the recreational areas set aside along this fabulous roadway.

Mile markers, or mile posts, can be seen each mile along the Overseas Highway. They appear on the right shoulder as small green signs with white numbers and begin with number 126 just south of Florida City. The mile markers end with the zero marker at the corner of Fleming and Whitehead streets in Key West (a favorite photo spot). When asking for

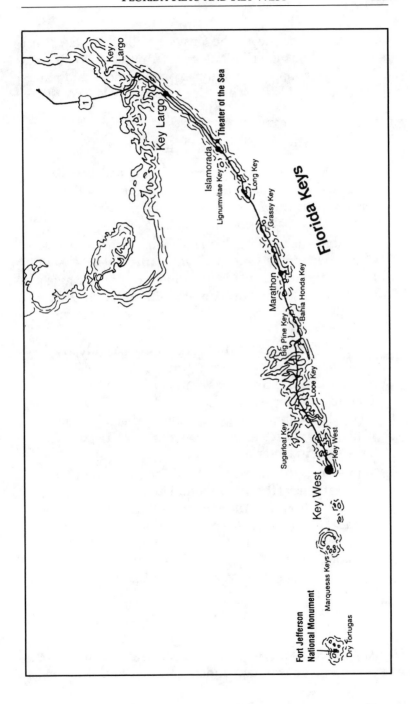

directions in the Keys, the answer will likely be, "Just before," or "Just after" a mile marker number. To obtain a complete vacation kit detailing accommodations and attractions in the Florida Keys and Key West, call 800-FLA-KEYS.

---

### A NOTE ON THE FOOD OF THE FLORIDA KEYS

Seafood! Glorious, glorious seafood! Giant-sized groupers, minuscule grunts, the incredibly good spiny lobster, pink shrimp and that succulent delight, stone crabs—all vie as best or most delicious dishes.

Among the meat items on the menu, lechon is a roast of pork wondrously flavored with garlic and those sour Key oranges. Vaca frita is literally fried cow, ropa vieja (old clothes) is a leftover meat dish, and then there's picadillo, a hamburger made with capers and raisins in a savory sauce.

Conch (pronounced konk) is king, particularly in Key West. You can order conch fritters, conch chowder, conch salad, and conch steak. You know those great big lustrous pink shells you see in shell shops? Those are conch shells, and you eat the mollusks that live in them. With your conch salad, try some chewy, crispy, squid rings fried in batter.

Dessert is the famed Key Lime Pie made from limes with that special flavor only found in the Keys. The lime trees came from the Yucatan, and they became famous in the Florida Keys. Pies are simple to make with condensed milk, but the juice and minced rind of those piquant Key limes make them a dessert to die for. No matter your pleasure, you'll find the Keys' cuisine a Lucullan delight.

---

**Key Largo.** (MM 100) Wildlife abounds in the Florida Keys, you just have to go under the water to observe most of it. An absolute must is the John Pennekamp Coral Reef State Park, MM 102.5, the first underwater park in the U. S. The residents here are fish—more than 300 species of them—and coral, along with twenty-seven species of gorgonians, or anemones. Pennekamp is like a visit to a small planet, and you need a space suit (scuba gear) or you can take a spaceship (a glass-bottomed boat). For those who want just a surface view, snorkeling boats leave twice a day. Out on the Key Largo Dry Rocks snorkelers and divers can see a nine-foot bronze statue of Christ, plus a four-foot barracuda that will pose for photographs.

Pennekamp has camping facilities, and for those visitors who don't care about the denizens of the deep, windsurfer and Hobie Cat rentals are available.

Avid Bogart fans will never forget this famous star and Lauren Bacall battling both Edward G. Robinson and a hurricane at the same time in the 1948 movie classic *Key Largo*. The island today hardly looks like moviegoers remember it from the Bogart-Bacall version. In fact, Key Largo, largest of the forty-three subtropical islands that make up the Florida Keys, is like any other small American tourist town with growing pains. Chain restaurants vie with dive shops, shell shops, and T-shirt shops for space on the highway, as large and small motels beckon tourists to stay for a day, a week, a month, or forever. You might check on the Largo Lodge with little apartments hidden in a tropical garden for a touch of the Bogart-Bacall era (305-451-0424). The Caribbean Club Bar near MM 104 claims that a few minutes of the movie were filmed there, but according to another legend, it was at a bar that has burned down. And, to further destroy the movie aura, locals say that only about three minutes of the film's footage were shot in Key Largo, because the stars and crew couldn't face the mosquitoes and sand fleas.

A visible legend of the Bogart era is the original *African Queen* on display at the Key Largo Holiday Inn (MM 100). British-built in 1912, she was christened *SL Livingstone* for the

*Remember the movie* Key Largo *with Bogart and Bacall? The Caribbean Club claims they were here.*

African river trade. She was discovered in 1951 on Lake Albert by Hollywood set designers seeking an authentic vessel for the movie. Charlie Allnutt and Rosie Sayer were portrayed by Bogart and Katharine Hepburn, who turned in magnificent performances and created a movie classic. Who can forget the scene when Rosie has to pick off the loathsome leeches embedded in Charlie's body?

Bogey won an Academy Award (his only one) for his role, but Hepburn did not. There are no awards given to props, but an exception should have been made for the *African Queen*. It captured the hearts of millions, and it really didn't blow up, as the movie would have you believe. That scene was filmed on a sound stage. After many many adventures and voyages, the old *Queen* was purchased by James W. Hendricks for its final dock at Hendricks' Holiday Inn Marina.

The new Key Largo Undersea Park (MM 103.5) is set in an acre-wide enclosed lagoon designed to emulate the ocean's natural ecology and environment. Here is an authentic hands-on undersea exhibit for snorkeling enthusiasts of all skills. A powerful filtering system purifies the lagoon at a rate of 1,200 gallons per minute providing divers with crystal-clear visibility up to fifty feet.

It's not 20,000 leagues under the sea, but at Jules' Undersea Lodge, the world's only underwater hotel, six guests can stay in a 50-ft × 20-ft steel and acrylic structure anchored thirty feet beneath the surface of the lagoon. You don't need music to lull you to sleep, the fish gliding by your window send you right to dreamland. An 8-ft × 20-ft multipurpose chamber serves as dining room and entertainment complex including television and computer games. Staff members will loan you an underwater video camera to record your visit, and "mermaid" service is also available. You select your own menu—right off the frozen food counter—and zap it in the community microwave. Rates are not in the bargain category, but remember, Captain Nemo never had it so good (305-451-2353).

Also part of the park, the MarineLab Undersea Habitat works on actual underwater research projects, and the "accretion project" is a watery studio where marine artists work with the sea to create unique and beautiful sculptures.

The quiet town of Tavernier (MM 93) is interesting with its old post office and Methodist Church. The "red cross house" (MM 93, oceanside) was built after the 1935 hurricane, and even the roof and floors were made of reinforced concrete. Harry Harris County Park (MM 92.5) has excellent beaches and picnic facilities.

**Windley Key.** Here at Theater of the Sea (MM 85.5) is paradise for all you Flipper lovers. You can watch the graceful dolphins cavort and perform for your enjoyment, and you can give that sleek rubbery skin an affectionate pat.

Theater of the Sea is the second oldest marine park in the world. When Henry Flagler built his railroad, he left behind massive gravel pits. Theater of the Sea, opened in 1946, has turned one of these pits into a huge tree-lined lagoon that has resulted in a natural ecosystem for the mammals. If

*The seals are well-balanced at Theater of the Sea.*

you've always wanted to touch a shark or pet a stingray, then you will enjoy Theater of the Sea even more. When one of the silly seals fails to come up for a tasty fish, the handler sings his favorite song, ''You Picked A Fine Time To Leave Me, You Seal.'' The owners also love and care for lost and stray cats, and even if you see a tabby you want to take home, they are not for adoption.

World-class sportfishing attracts many an angler to Upper and Lower Matecumbe Keys, and to Islamorada.

**Islamorada** (pronounced EYE-la-mor-AH-da) is the lovely centerpiece of a group of coral islands with the enticing name of "the purple isles" that include Plantation, Windley, Upper and Lower Matecumbe Keys. The Spanish word *morada* refers to the lovely violet sea snail, *Janthina Janthina*, found in abundance on the seashore. Or, perhaps it means the railroad vine or goatweed that lacily covers the islands in mulberry shades. Another (rather dull) translation is "homestead." Take your choice, Islamorada is worth a leisurely stopover.

Find that attractive wild spot behind the town library where a stream flows by mangroves and forms a perfect swimming hole with picnic tables nearby.

Offshore there's a Coral Underwater Sea Garden for snorkelers or scuba divers, and the area holds a reputation as one of the finest for tarpon and sailfish prizes. Islamorada is where George Bush goes out for the big ones, and this town calls itself "The Sportfishing Capital of the World." Mr. Bush checks in at the posh Cheeca Lodge.

Boat tours to Lignumvitae and Indian Keys leave from the boat ramp at MM 78.5. Indian Key is a State Historic Site with a gory past fraught with tales of wrecking, unscrupulous dealings by former owner Jacob Houseman, and Indian massacres. May is particularly nice on Indian Key. Not so much for the climate, but jillions of tiny white butterflies migrate here from South America. If you didn't know better, you would think a blizzard hit the island.

Lignumvitae Key is tamer: a State Botanical Site with 133 species of trees, including its namesake. The wood of the lignum vitae (wood of life) tree is so dense that it has been known to outlast steel and bronze. Here is the last remaining example of what the Florida pristine vegetation was all about. If you make this interesting side trip, take mosquito repellent.

Long Key State Recreation Area (MM 67.5) is one of the most popular camping areas on the Keys. With a swimmable beach, observation tower, boardwalk, and the Golden Orb Weaver Nature Trail, Long Key has it all. If you haven't guessed, the golden orb weaver is a spider, large but harmless. Author Zane Grey loved this spot, and when he retreated from Arizona and his western novels, he came here to fish. A creek bears his name.

**Marathon on Key Vaca.** (MM 50) Located midway down the Keys, Marathon deserves its appellation of "Heart of the Keys." Here you will find mid-America: shopping malls, country club, golf course, airport, and every possible chain store and chain restaurant. This busy city began as a base camp for the Flagler railroad, but now 11,000 people call Marathon home. Sportfishing is the primary industry, and tournaments are held throughout the year. A nice bed and breakfast called the Hopp Inn is popular with Marathon guests.

Archaeologists, whether amateur or professional, should make it a point to visit Crane Point Hammock (MM 50), one of the most important sites in the Keys. Here is evidence of pre-Colombian and prehistoric Bahamian artifacts. Crane Point Hammock is also an important environmental resource. On a nature walk visitors can learn about the red mangroves, called "walking trees" because their long roots give the tree a legged appearance. Mangroves are important in southern Florida as they are invaluable in the marine food chain and a massive hurricane barrier to a very slippery coastline. Destroying a mangrove tree can bring a $10,000 fine.

Just south of Marathon you cross the beautiful new Seven Mile Bridge, the longest segmental bridge in the world (6.79 miles). In April, runners arrive for the Seven-Mile Bridge Run in a race over the azure waters of the Atlantic Ocean and the Gulf of Mexico. Here is a vantage point unsurpassed for taking in the sheer sweep of the Straits of Florida and the Gulf of Mexico. The old bridge has now become a popular site for fishing.

On **Grassy Key** (MM 60) is another major facility where dolphins are studied year-round. At the Dolphin Research Center (MM 59) you can make a tax-deductible contribution to the survival of these wonderful creatures. The center accepts sick and wounded dolphins found in coastal waters, and it also accepts dolphins from other marine research facilities where the animals sometimes suffer from overcrowded conditions. Still more dolphins, "burnt out" from years of performing in aquariums, spend their "retirement" at the center and receive a complete rejuvenation. In their similarities to humans, stress has even resulted in bleeding ulcers in these gentle intelligent animals.

**Sunshine Key** (MM 39) is a refuge for pioneering types who crave living off the land at a 400-site camping resort just past the Ohio-Missouri Bridge.

**Bahia Honda Key** (MM 37) is the home of a state recreation area that has three camping areas with cabins, a dive shop, a marina, and picnic grounds. Its beach has been described as ''the best beach on the Keys.''

Bahia Honda has a number of plants that are not often found on the other islands. Among the rarer species are the satinwood tree, spiny catesbaea, and dwarf morning glory. You'll see all of the gorgeous Florida Keys' birds, and the tarpon fishing rates among the best in the state.

**Looe Key** (MM 30) One of the world's finest coral reefs is at Looe Key National Marine Sanctuary. Many divers prefer Looe Key to Pennekamp with Looe's old movie sites, bird hammocks, and abandoned shrimp plantations.

**Big Pine Key** (MM 31) is the home of a handful of tiny Key Deer, no larger than medium-sized dogs. These highly endangered deer are making a last-ditch stand against speeding cars, loss of browsing land, and garbage. The National Key Deer Refuge is at MM 30, but the little critters are hard to spot during midday.

**Sugarloaf Key.** At MM 17 stop for a look at the bizarre Perky Bat Tower behind Sugarloaf Lodge. It looks like a bladeless windmill just waiting for Don Quixote. Back in 1929 (this was before spray-on mosquito repellent), Clyde Perky, a kindhearted gentleman, wanted his guests to enjoy their visit at his lodge without the voracious attacks of hordes of mosquitoes. He built this strange tower and filled it with odorous bat guano to attract mosquito-eating bats, but in the ensuing battle, the mosquitoes won and Perky's fly-by-night scheme failed.

**Key West:** The last stop.

On the stairway of the Florida Keys, Key West is the top rung, even though it is only four feet above sea level. Spanish explorers said they found this place buried in human bones, a tale that may have led to its Spanish name of *Caya*

*Hueso*—Island of Bones. The unattractive name was eventually Anglicized into Key West, although a handful of keys still lie farther west.

Entering Key West for the first time is disappointing. Heading into the heart of Key West, North Roosevelt Boulevard takes you through all the modern rubble of chain motels, chain foodstores, chain shopping malls, and bumper-to-bumper traffic. Finally, you wind up on Duval Street, which bisects Old Town. Here is where it's at!

You don't refer to the local population as Key Westerners. A large part of Key West's history comes from its being a haven for transients from the ends of the earth, and its citizens even have a distinctive title—Conchs. The first Conchs were British sympathizers who fled the Thirteen Colonies during the American Revolution. Sailing under the slogan, ''We'd rather eat conchs than fight,'' they settled in the Bahamas, later migrating to Key West.

It is said by many old-timers you are not a true Conch unless you are a third generation Conch, born in Key West. But, if you live in Key West for at least seven years, you can be a ''Freshwater Conch.'' Or, even more prestigious is to become an ''Honorary Conch,'' a title bestowed upon one by the Monroe County Commission. Becoming an Honorary Conch acknowledges ''acceptance as an equal by the world's friendliest people, the Conchs.''

To make a concise and definite plan for experiencing Key West is as futile as making a concise and definite plan for getting out of a maze. Sure, there are specific sights to see, places to eat and stay, but you should follow some adventurous inclinations rather than a printed tour guide.

First, you need a place to hang your clothes. In this easy-going atmosphere, you'll get the impression that the fewer clothes you wear, the more you are in style. For posh quarters, it's The Pier House at the northern tip of Duval Street. However, if you want a real Bogart-Bacall atmosphere, head for The Reach. In nautical terms, ''the reach'' is a pause between journeys. With its pink walls, wide verandas, verdant gardens, and island decor, you expect to see Bogey and Bacall, arm in arm, strolling casually down the wide stairway. This hotel is truly perfect for Key West. Just around the corner are Southmost House and nearby Southmost Point—the most popular Key West photography spots.

*The most photographed place in the Florida Keys.*

Also in Old Town are a number of luxurious bed-and-breakfast accommodations in restored historic houses. Write the Chamber of Commerce for a listing. You can count on imaginative and attractive establishments.

The three most popular transportation methods are walking, bicycling, and motor scooters. At every corner is a bicycle and scooter rental, so take your choice. Or, how about these two good introductions to the scene: the venerable Conch Train, and its clone, the Old Town Trolley. Both roam the streets on ninety-minute tours, and you can choose where you want to walk, cycle, or scooter back and spend more time.

Every hour is the cocktail hour in Key West. So, stop at Captain Tony's Saloon, 428 Greene Street. The inside is rather hokey, with its walls papered in business cards, but this was the original Sloppy Joe's where Hemingway relaxed with a drink or a fight. It is also considered the oldest bar in Florida, but there's no historical marker proclaiming its distinction. The current Sloppy Joe's is only a few steps away at the corner of Greene and Duval. Hemingway also patronized this drinking establishment even when it had the tacky name of Midget Bar. "Papa" Hemingway memorabilia is about as rampant in Key West as slivers of the True Cross are in the Holy Land.

*The second most photographed place in the Keys.*

While you are doing a "Hemingway day," go on down to the Hemingway House on the corner of Whitehead and Olivia Streets. Hemingway bought it for $6,000 in 1931 and lived here for ten years. In between bar visits and deep sea fishing, "Papa" managed to turn out *For Whom the Bell Tolls*, *A Farewell to Arms*, and *The Snows of Kilimanjaro*. Hemingway's ex-secretary, Toby Bruce, swears that not one piece of the original furniture is in that house. Bruce also swears that the cats, even the ballyhooed seven-toed ones, belonged to a neighbor and not to "Papa." But, Hemingway's wife did build the swimming pool, and it did cost $20,000. When "Papa" returned from a trip and saw it, he was furious and threw in a penny with the angry rejoinder, "Here, you might as well have my last penny." The penny is still embedded in the pool's concrete.

The great, the near-great, and the never-heard-ofs have all walked Key West's narrow streets. Tennessee Williams, Gore Vidal, Carson McCullers, Jimmy Buffett, and Harry Truman are names that everyone will recognize. And, one of the most famous was John James Audubon. To see the Audubon House today, you would think he lived there for years, but the great artist was actually in residence only a few weeks. However, the house at Green and Whitehead is interesting because most of the antiques were hauled off sinking ships by wreckers.

A great deal of renovation has been done in Key West on the Conch Houses. As to just what a Conch House is, well, it must look like it belongs in Key West. It has gingerbread railings and expansive verandas. Shutters shade the windows, and cisterns catch fresh water. Small, square, roof hatches called scuttles let out hot air. Most are at least one hundred years old and usually built by ship's carpenters who had never designed homes before.

Strolling the streets and admiring Conch Houses makes a delightful day for history and architecture buffs. The Oldest House at 322 Duval is also open as a museum.

Key West underground is fascinating as well. The City Cemetery may well be the highlight of any "graver" that likes tombstones. One straightforward epitaph says it all with, "I told you I was sick." Another one, obviously chosen by a grieving widow, says, "At least I know where he's sleeping tonight." In Key West, the Conchs rely heavily on nicknames, so you'll find Bunny, Shorty, Lito, Bean K., and The Tailor.

But, these twenty-one acres of prime real estate in the heart of Key West's historic district are also a monument to a "small little war," as Teddy Roosevelt called it. Here rest the remains of those who died when the U. S. Battleship *Maine* was sunk in Havana's harbor in 1898. With so many bodies, and so little space, the Conchs have had to recycle graves and bury old skeletons deeper. Soon there may be 100,000 bodies buried in 15,000 spaces. Don't forget your camera when you tour City Cemetery.

You might want to check out the docks at the Truman Annex. Many of the 125,000 Cubans who fled their country in 1980 on anything that would float landed here at Key West. For a long time, "Would the last person to leave Cuba please turn out the lights" was written in Spanish above the large doors to the only building on Pier B.

The Trolley or Conch Train will take you by President Harry Truman's Little White House, President Kennedy's Bay of Pigs Invasion command post, the Lighthouse (dating back to 1846), the Art Museum, Martello Towers, and on a short jaunt on your own you can find Fort Zachary Taylor. Watch out for Conch mosquitoes.

End up at Mallory Square, because around this point is the most fascinating part of Key West. When wreckers were the mainstay of Key West economy in the 1830s, Mallory Square was the center of commerce.

Have you ever dreamed of finding pirate gold and becoming as rich as Croesus? Well, Mel Fisher did just that. Mel Fisher's Gold Exhibit at 200 Greene Street has treasures recovered from the Spanish galleon *Atocha*, which sank in

1622. Along with more than 150 pounds of gold are silver bullion, emeralds, diamonds, copper, brass cannons, rare antiques, and historic artifacts. All told, the treasure is worth more than $40 million.

First, see the movie that Fisher made describing the discovery. It will explain just how difficult it is to find sunken treasure. Then take a very slow walk through the museum: doubloons, gold bars, even a poison cup with a bezoar stone that changes color when it comes in contact with a toxic substance. Somebody on the *Atocha* must have had a lot of enemies. One of the gold chains on display weighs more than six pounds! If you have time for only one place to visit in Key West, it has to be the *Atocha* exhibit.

The first tourist attraction built in the Keys was the Key West Aquarium and it represents the first open-air aquarium in the United States. Built in 1932, the aquarium has come a long way. The living coral reef still in the experimental stage offers a fascinating view of a struggling coral system and the sea life that makes its home in such waters. A huge touch tank delights the younger set.

The Turtle Kraals (a Dutch/South African word for corrals) are a remnant of an old Key West industry: turtle slaughter. Now protected as an endangered species, these gentle creatures are merely on display, and a waterfront restaurant feeds them leftovers.

Shops of every shape, size, and description abound in Old Town. With bars, restaurants, Conch Houses, and wares from all parts of the world, Old Town takes days to explore. One brief afternoon will only whet your appetite for more.

Speaking of whetting your appetite, Key West abounds with fine restaurants, and the Chamber of Commerce will be delighted to give you a list of the ones it recommends. The list is long, and it's to be hoped that you will be staying in Key West long enough to try them all.

An hour before Key West puts on its best show—sunset— the place to be is Mallory Dock. The sun, usually a blazing globe of incredible orange, seems to drop off the edge of the universe. A Key West sunset is truly one of nature's spectacles, and the Conchs love to celebrate the fiery event every evening. And as for "calling it a day," Key West has added food vendors, sidewalk painters, fortune tellers, musicians, jugglers, mimes, a fire-eater or two, and a nice clean-cut guy that likes to lie down on a bed of nails—points up, of course. All of this nonsensical entertainment is free, but do be ready with a nice tip when the hat is passed. In other words, the Sunset Celebration is a circus, a zoo, an event, and definitely a must. A writer once wrote, "Across the rest of the world, the sun is asked merely to rise, shine, and set. In Key West it must perform."

*While waiting for the sunset, you can buy a T-shirt or a beach toy in Key West.*

**The Farther Keys.** The Overseas Highway may end, but the Keys go on. For a breathtaking view of the cobalt blue seas and a trip to fantasy islands (without Ricardo Montalban and Tattoo) charter a seaplane and really go to the end of the Keys. You'll see the Marquesas, a ring of islands that make up the only atoll in the Atlantic Ocean. On Rebecca Shoal a rusty ship marks the spot of treasure hunter Mel Fisher's discovery of the *Atocha*.

At the end of the thirty-five minute flight lie the Tortugas. You may think you are seeing the Lost City of Atlantis rising out of the sea, but actually it is only Fort Jefferson, the Gibraltar of the Gulf, or as it was once called, "Devil's Island of the Carribean." Construction began in 1846 and continued for thirty years, yet the fort was never completed. The octagonal structure with its eight-foot-thick walls rising fifty feet high covers most of the sixteen acres of Garden Key. (This Key must have gotten its charming name before Fort Jefferson was built.)

Occupied by Federal troops during the Civil War, the fort saw little action then or at any other time. After the Civil War it became a prison, and its inmates included four strange prisoners. These were the men linked to the assassination of Abraham Lincoln. The most famous was Dr. Samuel A. Mudd, an innocent victim who made the mistake of setting an unknown man's broken leg. Unfortunately for Dr. Mudd, the leg belonged to John Wilkes Booth. Mudd was sentenced to a life of hard labor. However, in 1867, a yellow fever epidemic struck Fort Jefferson, and for his tireless aid Dr. Mudd was pardoned two years later.

When you plan to stay a while on Garden Key for the snorkeling and scuba diving, be sure to bring your own water and buckets of mosquito repellent. You may even luck out and see the loggerhead turtles, for which Ponce de Leon named the Tortugas. Hunting has almost eliminated the loggerheads.

In April and early May, bird-watchers should go to Bush Key east of Fort Jefferson. For some reason known only to

Mother Nature, thousands of sooty terns come each year from as far away as West Africa to lay their eggs, hatch their young, and fly 9,000 miles back to West Africa. When they are four years old, they will find Bush Key and begin the cycle of life again.

On Loggerhead Key, you reach the very tip of Florida and a 130-year-old lighthouse. Here at the end of the Keys is truly splendid isolation. Few tourists ever venture this far, and you have the sun, the glistening white sand, the incredible turquoise water, and uninhabited islands all to yourself, unless, you decide to include someone special.

# INDEX

**A**

Adventures Unlimited, 31
*African Queen,* 157
Alcazar Hotel, 44
Alligator Alley, 113
Alligators, 117
Amelia Island, 40
Amelia Island Plantation, 42
Anna Maria Island, 71
Apalachicola, 17
Apopka, 64
Arcadia, 74
Aripeka, 59
Asolo State Theater, 73
Atocha, 168

**B**

Babcock Wilderness Adventure, 121
Babson Park, 101
Bahia Honda Key, 163
Banyan Tree, The, 76

Bardin, 51
Bartow, 96
Bartram, William, 49, 54
Basketville, 76
Bay Harbor Inn, 130
Beaches of South Walton, 34
Beal-Maltbie Shell Museum, 86
Belle Glade, 145
Bern's Steak House, 70
Big Pine Key, 163
Big Tree Park, 87
Biscayne National Park, 150
Black Hills Passion Play, 97
Blountstown, 20
Blue Springs State Park, 112
Boca Grande, 119
Boca Grande Lighthouse Park, 120
Bok Tower, 97
Bone Valley, 96
Branch Ranch, 70

Brooksville, 64
Busch Gardens, 65
Bush Key, 171
Butterfly World, 139

C

Cabbage Key, 118
Ca'd'zan, 72
Caladesi Island, 58
Calusa Lodge, 146
Cape San Blas, 18
Captiva Island, 118
Caribbean Club Bar, 157
Carrabelle, 16
Casa de Solana, 44
Casey Key, 77
Caspersen Beach, 76
Cassadaga, 108
Castillo de San Marcos, 43
Cedar Key, 24
Central East Florida, 103
Central Florida, 79
Central Florida Zoo, 87
Central West Florida, 55
Chalet Suzanne, 98
Charles Hosmer Morse
    Museum of American
    Art, 84
Chautauqua Winery, 34
Chiefland, 24
Chinsegut Hill National
    Wildlife Refuge, 64
Chipley, 37
Clermont, 93
Clewiston, 145
Clewiston Inn, 145

Club Continental, 51
Coldwater River, 31
Collier Automotive
    Museum, 124
Collier-Seminole State
    Park, 125
Columbia Restaurant, 44, 69

Conchs, 164
Coral Castle, 131
Coral Gables, 131
Corkscrew Swamp
    Sanctuary, 126
Crane Point Hammock, 162
Cross Creek, 52
Crown Hotel, The, 63
Cypress Gardens, 99
Cypress Knee Museum, 146

D

Dade Battlefield State
    Historic Site, 64
Daytona Beach-Cassadaga-
    De Leon Springs, 108
"DaVinci of debris," 75
Daytona Beach-Ponce Inlet
    Lighthouse, 106
Dead Lakes State
    Recreation Area, 20
DeFuniak Springs, 34
DeLand, 112
De Leon Springs State
    Park, 111
Dog Island, 16
Dolphin Research Center,
    162

Driftwood Inn, 104
Dunedin, 58

**E**

Eden State Gardens, 34
Edison Museum, 114
Everglades, 147
Everglades City, 125
Everglades National Park
Boat Tours, Inc., 125

**F**

Falling Waters State
Recreation Area, 37
Farther Keys, 171
Fernandina Beach, 41
Flamingo, 149
Flamingo Inn, 149
Florida Cactus, Inc. 88
Florida Citrus Tower, 93
Florida City, 151
Florida Cracker, 55
Florida House, 41
Florida Keys and Key West,
152
Florida Southern University,
95
Fort Clinch, 41
Fort Jefferson, 171
Fort Myers, 114
Fort Myers-Captiva
Island-Sanibel Island, 115
Fort Myers-Naples-
Everglades City, 122

Fort Myers-Port
Charlotte-Boca Grande,
118
Fort Pierce, 104
Fort San Marcos de
Apalachee, 15
Fountain of Youth, 42
Frostproof, 101
Fruit & Spice Park, 136

**G**

Gainesville-Rawlings
Home-Micanopy-
McIntosh, 51
Gamble Plantation, 71
Garden Key, 171
Gasparilla Inn, 120
Gasparilla Island, 119
Gatorland Zoo, 82
Gibson Inn, 18
Gold Coast, 130
Graceville, 35
*Grand Romance*, 87
Grassy Key, 162
Green Cove Springs, 51

**H**

Harrington House, 71
Hastings, 49
Havana, 21
Henry Plant Museum, 69
Herlong Mansion, 53
Highland Hammock, 101
Hillcrest Lodge, 101
History of Florida, 1

Homosassa Springs Wildlife Park, 63
Honeymoon Island, 58
Hontoon Island, 112
Hopp Inn, 162
Immokalee, 126
Indian Key, 161
Inn by the Sea, 123
Inverness, 63
Islamorada, 160
Izaak Walton Lodge, 24

**J**

Jacksonville-Amelia Island, 40
Jacksonville-Palatka (St. Johns River Drive), 47
Jacksonville-St. Augustine and Marineland, 42
Jim Hollis' Suwannee River Rendezvous, 25
J. N. "Ding" Darling National Wildlife Refuge, 115
John Hudson's Alligator Farm, 137
John Pennekamp Coral Reef State Park, 157
Jules' Undersea Lodge, 159
Jungle Larry's Safari and Caribbean Gardens, 124

**K**

Kenwood Inn, The, 44
Key Largo, 156

Key Largo Undersea Park, 158
Key Vaca, 161
Key West, 163
Koreshan State Historic Site, 122

**L**

Lakeland, 95
Lake Okeechobee, 129
Lakeridge Winery, 93
Lakeside Inn, 90
Lake Wales, 97
Lake Weir, 91
Largo Lodge, 157
Lightner Museum, 44
Lignumvitae Key, 161
Lion Country Safari, 141
Loggerhead Key, 172
Long Key State Recreation Area, 161
Longwood, 87
Looe Key, 163
Lower Matecumbe Key, 160

**M**

Mallory Square, 168
Malone, 35
Manasota Beach Club, 77
Manasota Key, 77
Manatee Springs State Park, 24
Manatees, 62
Mandarin, 47
Marathon, 161
Marco Island, 125

Marco Island Inn, 125
Marianna, 37
MarineLab Undersea
   Habitat, 159
Marineland, 45
Masaryktown, 64
Mayo, 25
McIntosh, 53
Mel Fisher's Gold Exhibit,
   168
Merrily, 53
Miami, 131
Miami-Clewiston-
   Okeechobee, 144
Miami Beach, 130
Micanopy, 53
Miccosukee Indian Village,
   142
Miller's Marina &
   Campground, 25
Milton, 30
Monkey Jungle, 135
Monticello, 26
Mt. Dora, 89
Mulberry Phosphate
   Museum, 97
Myakka River State Park, 73

**N**

Naples, 123
New Smyrna Beach, 103
Northeast Florida, 38
Northwest Florida, 11

**O**

Ocala, 91

Ochopee, 126
Oklawaha, 91
Old Saltworks Cabins, 19
Old South Bar-B-Q Ranch,
   145
Orange City, 112
Orange Park, 51
Orchid Jungle, 134
Orlando, 81
Orlando-Mt. Dora-Ocala
   (Silver Springs), 88
Orlando-Winter Park-
   Sanford-Wekiwa Springs,
   84
Ormond Beach, 104
Osprey, 75
Otter Springs RV Resort,
   25
Outdoor Resorts River
   Ranch, 101

**P**

Palatka, 49
Palmdale, 146
Panama Beach, 32
Panama City-Defuniak
   Springs-Marianna, 31
Park Plaza Hotel, 86
Parrot Jungle and Gardens,
   138
Pass-A-Grille, 56
Payne's Prairie State
   Preserve, 54
Peabody Hotel, 81
Peace River, 75
Pelican Inn, 16

Pelicans, 126
Pensacola-Milton, 29
Peppermill House, 27
Perry, 23
Picolata, 49
Pier House, The, 164
Pink Camellia, The, 18
Pinellas Suncoast, 55
Place St. Michael, 131
Plymouth, 88
Ponce de Leon Hotel, 44
Ponce de Leon Inlet
  Lighthouse, 106
Port Orange, 108
Port St. Joe, 18
Posey's, 15

**R**

Ravine Gardens, 50
Rawlings, Marjorie Kinnan,
  51
Reach, The, 164
Riverview Hotel, 103
Rookery Bay National
  Estuarine Research
  Reserve, 125
Roy's, 23

**S**

Saint Augustine, 42
Saint George Island State
  Park, 18
Saint Johns River Drive, 47
Saint Joseph's Peninsula
  State Park, 19
Saint Marks, 15

Saint Petersburg, 57
Saint Petersburg-Homosassa
  Springs-Inverness-
  Brooksville-Tampa, 56
Salvador Dali Museum, 58
Sanford, 87
Sanibel Island, 117
Santa Rosa Inn, 101
Sarasota, 71
Sarasota-Venice-Englewood,
  75
Scenic Boat Tours, 86
Seaside, 32
Sebring, 101
Selby Botanical Gardens, 73
Seven Mile Bridge, 162
Seven Sisters Inn, 93
1735 House, 41
Shell Factory, The, 115
Siesta Key, 73
Silver Springs, 92
Sloppy Joe's, 166
Southeast Florida, 129
Southmost Point, 165
Southwest Florida, 113
Spanish Oaks, 75
Spook Hill, 97
Spring hoppers, 23
Steinhatchee, 23
Stephen Foster State Folk
  Culture Center, 27
Sugar Mill Gardens, 108
Sugarloaf Key, 163
Suncoast Seabird
  Sanctuary, 58
Sunshine Key, 163
Suwannee River, 25, 28

Suwannee River State Park, 27

Switzerland, 49

**T**

Tallahassee-Apalachicola-Blountstown, 12
Tallahassee-Cedar Key, 21
Tallahassee-Havana, 21
Tallahassee-White Springs (Stephen F. Foster Memorial), 26
Tampa Bay Hotel, 68
Tampa-Sarasota-Arcadia-Zolfo Springs, 71
Tarpon Springs, 59
Tavernier, 159
Theater of the Sea, 159
Tocoi, 49
Torreya State Park, 20
Tortugas, 171
Treasure Coast, 104
Tupperware International Headquarters, 82
'Tween-Waters Inn, 118
Two Egg, 36

**U**

UDT-SEAL Museum, 104
Upper Matecumbe Key, 160

**V**

Venice, 76
Vero Beach, 104

**W**

Wakulla Springs, 14
Warm Mineral Springs, 77
Weeki Wachee, 59
Wekiwa Springs, 87
Wekiva River, 88
Wewahitchka, 20
White Springs, 27
Windley Key, 159
Winter Haven, 99
Winter Park, 84
Withlacoochee River, 64
Withlacoochee State Forest, 64
Wooten's Everglades Tours, 125
Wright, Frank Lloyd, 95

**Y**

Yankeetown, 24
Ybor City, 69
Yulee Sugar Mill Ruins, 63

**Z**

Zolfo Springs, 75